GARLIC

—The life-blood of— good health

STEPHEN FULDER PhD

THORSONS PUBLISHING GROUP

First published in 1989

British Library Cataloguing in Publication Data

Fulder, Stephen
Garlic.
1. Medicine. Herbal remedies. Garlic
I. Title
615'.324324

ISBN 0-7225-2132-4

*Published by Thorsons Publishers Limited, Wellingborough,
Northamptonshire, NN8 2RQ, England*

Typeset by Harper Phototypesetters Limited, Northampton
Printed in Great Britain by Biddles Limited, Guildford, Surrey

1   3   5   7   9   10   8   6   4   2

——Acknowledgements——

I would like to thank John Blackwood, who has worked with me on this garlic book as on our previous one, for his careful, thoughtful and literate attention to the manuscript. I would also like to thank Hofels Pure Foods Limited for their helpful technical information.

———Note to readers———

Before following the self-help advice given in this book, readers are urged to give careful consideration to any health problem they may have and to consult a competent practitioner. This book should not be regarded as a substitute for professional health care treatment. While every care is taken to ensure the accuracy of the contents, the author and publishers cannot accept legal responsibility for any problem arising out of the use of the methods described. This book is intended as general information about health, not as providing prescriptions for specific health problems.

Contents

L'ail est la santé. Mangez de l'ail!
Garlic is health. Eat it!

Introduction

Today we find garlic on the shelves of almost every pharmacy and health shop. It is given as much prominence as any modern remedy. Major articles on its health benefits have appeared in international newspapers and magazines and, most significantly, in the scientific and medical journals, from *Scientific American* to *The Lancet*. A recent book lists nearly one thousand scientific papers on the subject of garlic.

Of course, there is nothing new about its use as a medicine. It is one of the oldest known remedies of our civilization, used uninterruptedly for a wide variety of purposes until a century ago. Only during that relatively short period of time did it disappear from common use, along with most herbs, in favour of synthetic drugs. Now, however, it is being rediscovered. We are coming to realize that its benefits are highly relevant to some of the most widespread health problems of our time.

First and foremost, garlic is a preventive remedy against heart disease. This forms the major topic of our book and will be investigated thoroughly in its various aspects. Tradition says that it protects the circulation and thins the blood, and a considerable body of modern, scientific research has confirmed the traditional picture. Garlic lowers the levels of fat and cholesterol in the blood, and it does this as well as or better than the modern drugs now used for the purpose. An excess of fat and cholesterol is one of the major causes of the build-up of arterial blockages, and so of heart disease, heart attacks and strokes. It has been demonstrated that garlic 'thins' the blood by reducing its tendency to clot inside the blood vessels. Such clots are one of the causes of heart attacks, angina and strokes.

Thus garlic offers a double protection, something which no modern remedy is able to provide. Yet it is a safe medicinal food and has no significant side-effects. When it is made a part of a self-care regimen for protecting the heart (involving general diet, exercise and a more sanguine approach to daily life) it can make a real and vital contribution to the prevention of heart disease.

The other central use of garlic is in the prevention and treatment of infections. It has been found effective at killing a number of harmful bacteria and fungi. Extensive laboratory tests have shown that, though it is milder and less potent than modern antibiotics, it has a broader range of action than any of them and is, of course, safer. So garlic can play an important role in the self-treatment of chronic and less immediately severe infective problems. These include infections of the mouth, throat and chest, that is to say colds, coughs, catarrh, bronchitis, laryngitis and so on; infections of the stomach, such as 'holiday tummy' and gastroenteritis; infections of the skin, such as athlete's foot or ringworm; and infections of the urino-genital areas, such as thrush or cystitis. It may be particularly effective against Candida, a growing modern problem. For best results, though, garlic should be combined with other methods of self-care.

We should also take into account garlic's qualities as a flavouring and as a nutritional component of the diet, enjoyed today by a large proportion of the world's population. It is still medicinally effective when crushed and taken in food, though a significant amount, in the region of a couple of cloves, should be taken.

Garlic's botanical name is *Allium sativum*. This tells us that it belongs to the *Allium* group of plants in which there are some six hundred species. These include the onion, chives, leek, wild garlic, shallot, rakkyo, kurrat and various other ornamental and wild species. They all belong to the Lily Family. Garlic, like most of the members of this family, has spear-like leaves, about 15cm (6 inches) long. (Its English name comes from this; it is the Anglo Saxon *gar-leac*, or spear-plant.) These leaves originate from a fleshy base, or clove. From eight to twenty cloves are clustered together to form a bulb, which has a thin papery cover (Fig. 1). It also has a stem which, like the onion, sometimes produces purple-white flowers. The plant is grown from its own clove. This should be placed, tip uppermost, 5cm (2 inches) under the soil, the best time being at the end of November. The plant will then emerge in late winter, grow throughout the spring and be ready for harvest in the summer. The fleshy substance of the clove provides food and sustenance while it is developing, and its pungent content, which we humans rely on as food

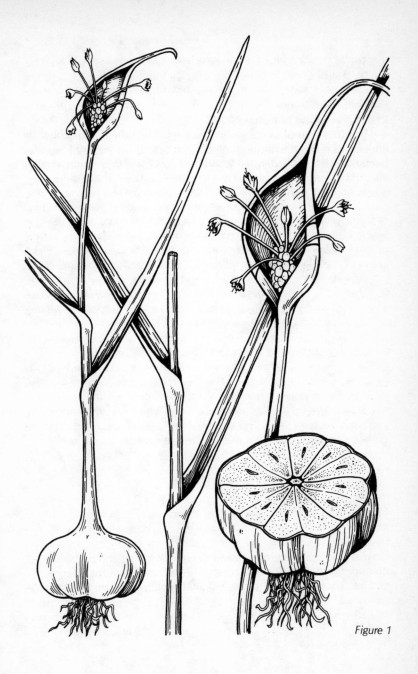

Figure 1

and medicine, also provides its own chemical defence system, warding off pests and diseases while it grows beneath the soil.

Garlic does indeed contain some remarkably strong and unusual substances. What is it that can keep the arteries open, can kill bacteria, yeasts and fungi, can heat the body and drive out poisons, and can even kill insects, all at relatively small dosages and without being harmful to people? The key to garlic's potency is found in one element: sulphur. Even more than the other alliums, garlic has the ability to accumulate some very unusual sulphur compounds. You might have guessed it, considering its characteristic aroma and somewhat hellish reputation.

After several decades of research, scientists now have a good idea of the sulphur compounds in garlic which are of medicinal interest. The whole clove is rich in a substance called *alliin*, which hardly smells or tastes. As soon as it is crushed or chopped, a reaction begins which quickly changes the alliin into another compound called *allicin*. This smells strongly, has a pungent, fiery taste and is very active as a medicine.

After crushing, garlic becomes a veritable witch's brew of substances. The allicin is so reactive that it changes of its own accord into a range of other sulphur compounds, mainly *sulphides*, which have a strong, rich aroma. These sulphides are the principal active ingredients of garlic oil and cooked garlic and they too are medically effective.

Garlic, with its sulphurous nature, is clearly both fierce and friendly. There is an ancient legend to that effect. Having brought about the Fall of Man, Satan stepped from the Garden of Eden; where his right foot first rested, the onion plant sprang up, and where his left foot met the ground, there grew garlic. This dual quality of cursing and blessing typifies garlic's pungent power. Let us see how we can make best use of it.

CHAPTER 1

Heart disease and garlic eaters

In pursuit of a paradox

Whether you take the advice of a cardiac specialist or a modern naturopath, you will be told that a rich fatty diet, eating a great deal of animal products and drinking large quantities of coffee are all hazardous practices for the circulation. However, if you travel to the South of France, to Italy or to Spain, you will find an avid meat consumption, plenty of fatty, oily food and not much guilt about coffee. By rights, the lovers of *haute cuisine* and the portly Italian and Spanish bourgeoisie should be at the top of the heart disease league table.

The fact is that they are not. They are towards the bottom. The level of heart disease in thin Finns is higher than in fat French. Scotland has the highest level of all and England is next in the league table. As you move from Northern to Southern Europe, there is a very clear decrease, diet notwithstanding. Greece, and especially Crete, are level with the Japanese in having the least heart disease of all modern, developed nations.

In looking for explanations, scientists first came up with the observation that drinking wine, as opposed to beer or spirits, might be good for the heart, since those countries which drink more of it have lower levels of heart disease. This provoked a series of letters in the leading medical journal, *The Lancet*. Some doctors who were familiar with the Mediterranean suggested that, since wine drinking and garlic eating go together there, it could be the latter which kept heart disease at bay. Following this, a thorough and careful analysis was made by statisticians at the University of Western Ontario in Canada. They confirmed that the more garlic a nation consumed, the less heart disease there was among its population. They also found that the same thing was not true for wine.

This is impressive. Nevertheless, the scientists admitted that it could be the health-giving sun, the eating of olive oil or some other, unknown factor which was reducing heart disease in Mediterranean countries. What do the people of the South of France or Spain have to say? What do they believe is their secret? If you ask them, they will tell you that garlic is the answer. After centuries of experience, they acknowledge garlic as the protector of their arteries. Indeed, many of them see its use in cooking as having been developed specifically to balance the diet and neutralize the harmful residues from the quantities of fats consumed. One can observe similar combinations of customs in other nations outside the Mediterranean area: the Koreans, for example, eat a lot of meat and take a great deal of garlic with it.

Of course, this kind of observation remains vague and difficult to prove conclusively. To get more definite results, it would be necessary to take at least two groups of people who have similar lifestyles, except that one group eats garlic and the other does not. One could then measure differences in their health and physical state. In the 1970s, Dr Sainani and his colleagues at the Sassoon General Hospital in Pune, India, had the idea of conducting a study of this type among the Jain community. All Jain families have similar vegetarian diets, except that some are accustomed to eating onion and garlic, while others traditionally abstain from them. Dr Sainani assembled three groups of Jains who ate very smilar amounts and types of food. However, in one group each member had a weekly consumption of at least 600g of onion and 50g of garlic (this comes to around 17 cloves, a fairly substantial quantity). The second group took a weekly average of 200g of onion and 10g of garlic, while the third group ate none at all. It turned out that the amounts of cholesterol and fat in their blood matched their garlic and onion consumption very closely. The heavy garlic eaters had 25 per cent less cholesterol than the garlic avoiders. Since research has shown that a 10 per cent drop in blood cholesterol reduces the risk of a heart attack by 20 per cent, this is a major difference.

The drama of garlic research

As soon as scientists became aware that garlic might have a preventive action against heart disease, they began to test it in the laboratories. The first experiments were conducted at the Tagore Medical College, Rajasthan, India; at the University of Kerala, India; at Kyoto University,

Japan; at the University of Wisconsin, USA, and at the Alcorn State University, Mississippi, USA. It became obvious that feeding garlic to animals in a normal state of health could reduce both the amounts of fat and of cholesterol in the blood, often by as much as a quarter. As we shall see, cholesterol is known to be one of the factors which cause the blood vessels to become blocked, so leading to heart disease. The scientists found that, if garlic was added to the diet, more cholesterol was removed in the intestine during digestion and less was manufactured in the liver.

More comprehensive experiments were carried out on animals. Whatever one may think of the morality of such procedures, they are an inevitable part of modern experimental practice and they showed significant results. Rats, rabbits and other laboratory animals were fed fat-rich diets with the result that the cholesterol and fat levels in their blood and organs immediately rose to levels which, in humans, lead to heart disease. In the same way, the animals began to have problems with their circulatory systems. However, if garlic was fed to them at the same time as the fatty diet, the levels hardly rose at all and the harmful build-up in the circulation was stopped.

These observations caused a real excitement in the scientific world. Scientists from many different countries began to take a serious interest in garlic. They saw the possibility of a safe, natural preventive remedy which man could use to help resist the pressures put by modern life on the circulatory system. Trials began on human subjects, principally in India and subsequently in Europe. To date almost a thousand people have taken part in some twenty clinical studies. Some of them were patients with abnormally high blood cholesterol or blood pressure, and with various kinds of heart problem. Garlic proved itself dramatically. It appeared as effective as regular medical drugs, and a good deal safer, at reducing the level of fats in the blood. It also lowered blood pressure and reduced some of the symptoms caused by obstructions in the circulation, such as dizziness, chest pains and problems with blood flow to the legs.

Research has also shown that garlic is very effective at thinning the blood. In this it has a similar action to aspirin, which is often used for that purpose today. It reduces the tendency of the blood to build up clots within its own vessels. These blood clots, sometimes known as thromboses, are the major cause of heart attacks and strokes. Studies on this were carried out at the Universities of New York State and Washington, DC; at the Medical Research Council laboratories in Oxford;

at the University of Munich and in many other places. They showed that shortly after eating garlic the blood becomes noticeably thinner and less sticky. Further research was carried out in which various pure, chemical components of garlic were isolated. There is a current effort to produce a new anti-blood clotting pill based on one or more of them.

Scientific research has shown, then, that garlic lowers the amount of cholesterol and fat in the blood and the organs; that it helps to avoid atherosclerosis, the blocking of the arteries by fatty deposits; and that it keeps the blood thin, thus preventing strokes, coronary thrombosis, and unwanted blood clots in the vessels. These effects are the essential theme of this book and each one will be developed in more detail in later chapters.

The popularity of garlic as a remedy against heart disease

In recent years there has been a dramatic and worldwide increase in garlic's medicinal status. Backed by so much scientific research, the message of its significance has got through. Since heart disease is now the major cause of death in developed nations, the public have been searching for natural remedies which will help the heart harmlessly. Doctors too have shown increasing interest. There are regular medical drugs available which can reduce the amount of cholesterol in the blood. However, they are not without their side-effects and the doctors have been reluctant to prescribe them too widely. Moreover, since around two-thirds of the population in Britain and the USA have cholesterol levels above the optimum (that is to say, above 5.2 mmol/l, or 200mg/100ml), the drugs would have to be given to two out of three people. Understandably, most doctors are reluctant to turn the majority of the population into patients.

The natural answer is garlic. When I was giving a talk on British radio, the compere told me that he had been to see a specialist at a major teaching hospital in the UK about his heart. He told the specialist that he was a non-smoker, reasonably fit and a modest eater. What could he do to reduce the risk of a heart attack? The advice was, relax and eat garlic.

This advice has certainly been taken to heart in Germany. After a thorough review of the evidence, the Drugs Commission of the German Health Ministry recently announced that garlic is a medicine 'for assisting in the dietary treatment of raised blood fat levels' and for 'preventing age-related deterioration of the circulation'. Garlic is not so much a natural part of the German diet and many people prefer to take it in the form of garlic oil and other products. Its popularity there as a medicine is indeed astonishing. Nearly one million Germans now regularly take garlic products, mostly as a prevention against heart disease.

In the United States, a garlic product launched in 1982 achieved sales worth some $20 million within two years. In Japan, garlic preparations are accepted by the Health Ministry as a means of reducing blood pressure. Garlic appears in the official drug guides (or pharmacopoeiae) of other countries, including Spain and Switzerland. It is clear that it is a highly popular natural medicine, widely accepted throughout the world and steadily becoming acknowledged by the medical authorities.

Similar developments are taking place in the UK, where about 300 million garlic perles (capsules) are consumed a year. According to a recent poll, 10 per cent of the British population have used garlic or garlic products for medicinal purposes. The UK medical authorities have not yet accepted that garlic is effective in circulatory problems. They have, however, acknowledged its other main popular use, that of combating infections. Much of the consumption of garlic products in the UK occurs for infections of the stomach, throat, mouth, chest and urogenital area, and in this, too, as we shall see, there is backing from scientific research. The UK Ministry of Health allows the product manufacturers to claim that garlic is 'a herbal remedy traditionally used for the treatment of the symptoms of common cold and cough' and 'a herbal remedy traditionally used for the temporary relief of symptoms of rhinitis and catarrh'. This is cautious; however, it does show that the UK's leading drug experts realize garlic's medicinal potential.

CHAPTER 2

Understanding heart disease

The modern epidemic

The present day has opened a new chapter in the long history of garlic as a medicinal remedy. As we shall see in chapter 9, the herbalists of the past knew something of its beneficial effect on the blood, though this was not the most important of its uses. Now we know a great deal more, and that knowledge has become of extreme importance to us. For our greatest failing in the field of health is our inability to control the diseases of the heart and circulation, which now claim more lives than any other single cause. We need to understand, then, how heart disease arises and how garlic can be used in our daily lives, together with other precautions, to keep it in check.

The first thing we need to realize is how much heart disease is a thing of our own making. It is a modern problem which arises from two main general causes. The first is that almost all of us now live to an age at which diseases which build up slowly, over a period of time, are able to show themselves. Consider the fact that a hundred years ago, three-quarters of the population of Europe would not have reached their seventieth birthdays. Today, only one in three fails to make it. The big killers used to be the infectious diseases - tuberculosis, diphtheria, venereal disease, cholera and septicaemia. After they had been subdued, largely through developments in public health and sanitation, life expectancy increased considerably. However, the victory was only partial. The way was then left open for new kinds of disease - the degenerative conditions of mid- and later-life, in particular the diseases of the circulation and cancer. Because of them, a 40-year-old man today is no more likely to reach old age than was a 40-year-old man at the turn of the century. In the UK, they cause four out of every five deaths in middle age. Of the two, circulatory disease is the worse killer, outstripping even cancer.

Heart disease has now reached enormous proportions, striking at younger and younger age groups. Reviewing the situation in 1969, the World Health Organization predicted the coming of the greatest epidemic ever to face mankind. That epidemic is now fully upon us. In Britain, where the situation is at its worst, it is currently responsible for about half of all deaths.

——How the circulation becomes disordered——

In order to understand how garlic and other measures can help the circulation, we should consider how problems build up. The same basic process underlies all circulatory disorders. It begins with the gradual blocking or furring up of the arteries. Like a drain that slowly becomes blocked by accumulating layers of solids, so the arteries collect streaks of fat and more solid, fatty lumps on their inside surfaces. This occurs especially at certain key sites, for example at the places where the vessels divide and branch.

This is the palpable sign, the tip of the iceberg of an invisible process going on all the time within the metabolism. It may start with slight damage to the artery lining, which precipitates the first stage of the repair mechanism. Small cell pieces called platelets (which are the advance guard of the clotting process) arrive and stick to the damaged area; these act as flags and attract other cells involved in clotting. Cholesterol globules, always present in the bloodstream, join the platelets and form a spot or clot on the arterial lining. House-cleaning, scavenger cells migrate to the area. They attempt to clean up but in doing so they become so engorged with the excessive amounts of cholesterol present that they remain as fatty lumps; they are like a vacuum cleaner which becomes so overstuffed that it breaks down. More and more cholesterol accumulates at the site and the result is a fatty deposit or *plaque*. In time, the deposits so swell the interior surfaces of the blood vessels that the passageway becomes partially blocked. The blockage is called a *sclerosis* and the process of blockage is known as *atherosclerosis*.

Atherosclerosis increases with age and time and to some degree exists in all adults. When severe, it can itself precipitate the blood clotting mechanism normally reserved for sealing up breaks, as the body regards the narrowed vessels themselves as damaged and in need of repair. A clot which forms inside a vessel is called a *thrombosis*. The vessels that seem to be most at risk are those that bring the blood to the hardest working muscle in the whole body, the heart. These are called the coronary vessels. A clot that dams up these vessels is therefore called a *coronary thrombosis*. It stops blood from reaching the heart, causing chest pain, *angina*, or if more severe, a *heart attack*.

Other blood vessels which are particularly vulnerable are those of the brain, and if a thrombosis occurs in these it can lead to a *stroke*. Heart attack and stroke are the most common results of atherosclerosis. However, there can be other results, such as an increase in the blood pressure.

The inside investigation

We are most interested in understanding the origins of this process and the factors which will make the situation worse or better. We need to discover methods which will reduce the risk of heart attacks and other serious conditions. The questions we must ask are: can atherosclerosis be stopped and reversed, and if so, what kinds of remedies and preventive methods can be used and how genuinely reliable and effective are they?

The very first indications as to the causes of the process were obtained from a study not of the sick but of the healthy. Ever since 1948, thousands of inhabitants of the town of Framington in Massachusetts, USA, have been giving a detailed picture of their lifestyle to investigators from the US National Heart, Lung and Blood Institute. The researchers also checked them at regular yearly intervals for heart disease. Gradually the picture emerged that those most likely to suffer from heart disease were also more likely to be eating a lot of animal fat, to be smoking cigarettes, and to have raised blood pressure.

At first neither the health authorities nor the scientists took much notice of these findings. The prevailing view was that diseases were caused by outside agencies like bacteria and not by the way we lived. Over twenty years or so, however, the evidence accumulated. It became clear that those of the world's peoples who still lived in the traditional way without packaged, processed foods and with diets free of fatty meat - for example the Bedouin, the Aborigines and the Masai - never suffered at all from heart disease, unless they began to live in the modern way. It emerged that, as the nature practitioners had said all along, heart disease was the result of a variety of separate causes and that these could be summed up in two words: living unnaturally.

Enormous research projects, studying the life habits of hundreds of thousands of people, were carried out at a cost of hundreds of thousands of dollars. Various specific factors were identified as the main causes of heart disease. These were: a high proportion of animal fats in the diet; smoking; high blood pressure; diabetes and problems with sugar metabolism; being overweight, and also stress. There are other likely factors, such as deficiencies of certain vitamins and minerals about which naturopaths have always known and which are now coming to light. However, those given above were the ones shown by the research programme.

Stress is a profound problem. It was found that people who were tense, over-conscientious and under strain had a much higher chance of incurring heart attacks, even if they did not indulge themselves in cream buns and hamburgers. This psychological dimension, along with other factors such as food quality and lack of exercise, was seen as one of the reasons why our ancestors were not so often bedevilled by heart disease, despite a fat-laden diet.

Reaching a verdict on cholesterol

All the indicators now pointed to raised cholesterol levels in the body as one of the main direct causes of heart disease. Cholesterol is a type of fat needed by the body as the starting point in the manufacture of a variety of important materials. It is absorbed from the diet and also made by the liver.

The amount of cholesterol in the blood is influenced by several factors. The more cholesterol there is in the diet, the more there will be in the blood. The consumption of so-called saturated fats (the types of fat found in all animal and dairy products) encourages the liver to make more cholesterol. So, too, does stress and the production of adrenalin (the blood of racing drivers after a race becomes milky with fat droplets). Large amounts of fat stored up in the body, diabetes, and a lack of dietary fibre also increase cholesterol levels. Finally, for unknown reasons, some people have a hereditary tendency to higher levels than normal.

The amount of cholesterol in the blood is closely linked to atherosclerosis and heart attacks. Indeed, the UK National Institute of Health recently announced that cholesterol is not only a risk factor, it is actually a central cause of the problem.

The highest level of cholesterol in the world used to occur in East Finland at 6.9 millimols (mmol) to every litre (l), or 265 milligrams (mg) to every 100 millilitres (ml), of blood. The heart attack level there was fourteen times greater than the place with the lowest level, Japan, which had an average of 4.1 mmol/l, or 160mg/100ml. Proportionally, cholesterol levels have a very large influence on heart disease: a 10 per cent reduction in cholesterol brings down the incidence of disease by 20 per cent. In America, the average blood cholesterol has gone down a relatively small amount in the last few years, but heart attacks have been reduced by a third and the average lifespan has increased by three years.

In the UK there has been very little change in diet, lifestyle, cholesterol levels or heart attack rates. Life expectancy is lower than it is in the USA, and Britain - truly the sick man of Europe - has the unenviable reputation of being the country with the highest level of heart disease in the world.

The World Health Organization has looked at cholesterol levels worldwide and has stated that, for cardiac health, they should be at a maximum of 5.2 mmol/l, or 200mg/100ml. Unfortunately, two thirds of the adult population of modern, post-industrial countries are above this figure. This is a serious situation. Some medical authorities suggest that all such people should be given cholesterol-lowering drugs. This is surely absurd. It would turn the majority of adults in developed countries into patients, greatly enriching certain drug companies at everyone's expense and opening a Pandora's box of possible side-effects. Worst of all, it would divert effort away from taking the natural preventive measures which are within everyone's reach.

The fine tuning: LDL and HDL

Before we can understand how to improve cholesterol levels, we must deepen our knowledge of how it is handled within the body. It does not simply float around in oily drops. Each tiny droplet is contained within a bag of protein which makes it dissolvable in the blood. There are several types of cholesterol bag, but the ones that concern us here are called LDL (Low Density Lipoprotein) and HDL (High Density Lipoprotein). Between them, these carry 90 per cent of the cholesterol in the blood.

The liver makes cholesterol and sends it out to the fat stores. There some is taken up, and the rest circulates freely in the blood in the LDL form. The cells of the body all need small amounts of cholesterol. They take in some of the LDL, remove its cholesterol and leave the rest free. The more cholesterol that enters the bloodstream, the sooner the cells are satisfied and the more LDL remains in the blood.

LDL is in fact the 'bad' form of cholesterol. It is the one which is taken up by the arteries to create fatty lumps. It is also the most abundant. When cholesterol levels are measured, most is present in the form of LDL. So LDL levels are in fact more directly related to the risk of heart attack than those of cholesterol overall. Saturated fats, excess cholesterol in the diet, and smoking all increase LDL.

High Density Lipoprotein (HDL), on the other hand, may actually provide a protection against heart attacks. It has now been found that people with high levels of HDL are protected from heart disease even if their overall cholesterol is high. It seems to act as a kind of house-cleaner, collecting the cholesterol from the walls of the arteries and returning it to the circulation. For these reasons, the HDL/LDL ratio is very often used as a measure of cardiovascular risk: the higher it is, the better.

Clotting and coagulation

As we have seen, a heart attack or stroke is precipitated by a blood clot which forms in the blood vessel. This occurs when the clotting mechanism is triggered by the presence of a fatty area rather than, as is usual, by a break or wound. The mechanism is a complex cascade of actions and reactions. It originates with sticky cell fragments called *platelets* which circulate in the blood. As soon as they meet the rough edge of a wound or other damage, they clump together. At the same time, they release an agent which converts a blood protein, *fibrinogen*, to a fibrous material called *fibrin*. This forms a mesh over the area, in which the blood solidifies, so forming the clot.

However, there must be an opposite process which puts a brake on the clotting, otherwise it would continue and block the blood system every time it repaired a cut. This de-clotting, or breaking of the fibrin threads, is called *fibrinolysis*, and when it occurs inside the blood vessels it prevents the building up of clots.

The balance between fibrin formation and fibrinolysis affects the rate at which clotting takes place. A clot normally forms within several minutes. If there is more fibrin being made, it tends to form more quickly. More fibrinolysis, on the other hand, delays clotting, removes unwanted clots and generally thins the blood. Clearly it is very important to have this mechanism in good shape in order to prevent thromboses in the furred-up arteries.

Raised LDL-cholesterol levels increase fibrin and clot formation and reduce fibrinolysis. Adrenalin, the hormone poured into the blood during stress, also speeds up clotting and this adds to the chances of a heart attack in those under permanent psychological stress. Tobacco smoke, saturated fats and lack of exercise have the same effect. On the other hand, diets with the right kinds of fats can promote the fibrinolytic, clot-dissolving activity.

There is a further important dimension to the clotting process. This is the 'local messenger service' situated in the walls of the arteries. It dispatches substances which either promote the clumping of platelets and blood clotting (the messenger in this case is a prostaglandin called *thromboxane A₂*) or prevent clumping, reduce clotting and open blood vessels (achieved by *prostacyclin*). Since these chemical messengers are also made from the raw material of the fats we eat, we can promote the prostacyclin, clot-preventing system by dietary means.

Fish oil, in particular, contains a substance called EPA (eicosapentanoic acid). Our ancestors used to get EPA from wild animals. The flesh of domestic animals does not contain it, so it is present in our diet only in fish. When Dr Hugh Sinclair, the famous Oxford nutritional expert, went to live with the Eskimos and tested their exclusively fishy diet, the types of fats in his bloodstream greatly improved. He also suffered from nosebleeds and spontaneous wounds because of a reduction in clotting. However, we need not go as far as he did. EPA-rich, natural fish oil supplements have now become a very popular and medically approved method of reducing cholesterol in the blood and preventing unwanted clotting.

The remedy in the diet

Hundreds of studies have demonstrated that animal fats have the unfortunate result of increasing cholesterol, LDL, and blood clotting. This is now well accepted. However, that is not all. The total fat content of the diet contributes to the problem and should be decreased. In Japan, which has the lowest heart disease level of all developed countries, dietary fat makes up around 12 per cent of the total intake, whereas in the UK the percentage is three times as high.

At birth a human baby has some 1.3 mmol of LDL-cholesterol per litre of blood or 50mg/100ml, and this is the level at which the system is in balance. Yet in Western countries the normal adult LDL level is 3.2 mmol/l, or 125mg/100ml. It is possible to drop LDL back to its original level. It has been found that a pure vegan diet with no dairy products, no eggs or meat, will achieve it. Though few will be able to reach this goal, vegetarians as a whole have much less LDL, together with more HDL and, of course, a lower likelihood of cardiovascular problems.

A study of 24,000 non-smoking Seventh Day Adventists compared those who were vegetarian and those who were not and found that the meat-eaters were three times more likely to incur a heart attack than the vegetarians. Vegetarians have more fibre in their diet. This too helps the arteries, for fibre absorbs fat and bile like a sponge as it passes through the digestive system and removes it from the body. In fact the liver makes bile as one way of getting rid of cholesterol.

Both sugar and alcohol become converted to fat by the liver. Years of excessive alcohol or sugar consumption keep the liver producing excess fat and sending it out into the circulation for storage. Fasting or partial fasting is a well-tried method of ridding the body of extra fat, aiding the health of the circulation and removing toxins. A general regime for a healthy circulation will be given in more detail in chapter 5.

Positive constituents of the diet include leafy vegetables, fruit, and nuts and seeds. Fish and fish oil provide protein and are kind to the circulation. Whole grains are healthier than their refined counterparts (a cholesterol-lowering 'drug' has been isolated from barley by scientists at the University of Wisconsin). Spices and herbs are the best of all additions to the diet, and they also lower cholesterol. It is, after all, among them that we find – garlic.

Garlic, as we shall see in the following chapters, has the most wide-ranging and beneficial effect of all on the processes described above. It significantly reduces the levels of cholesterol in the blood, especially that carried by the harmful, low density lipoproteins, and it also increases the blood's tendency to dissolve clots. It seems tailor-made to help us in the dangerous position in which we now find ourselves, yet it is a natural and pleasurable part of our diet.

CHAPTER 3

Garlic and cholesterol

Garlic and butter

In an earlier chapter evidence was given to suggest that the nations which eat garlic do not share in the heart attack epidemic affecting the Northern Europeans and English language-based cultures of the world. We also pointed to the extensive and growing body of scientific evidence which substantiates this general claim. In this part of our book, we will examine this scientific evidence in more detail and consider its implications for our health and way of life.

Modern scientific research necessarily involves the use of animals at an early stage. The study of animals with heart disease has told us most of what we know about it and confirmed many of the ideas for its treatment, including the use of garlic. Sadly, it is all to easy to make an animal atherosclerotic - one only has to feed it a typical modern diet, with plenty of butter and fatty meat. All the usual changes result - furring of the arteries, heart damage and so on.

Garlic has been tested extensively on animals. The first observations were made in 1933 by scientists in Eastern Europe who wanted to test the local belief that taking garlic stopped atherosclerosis in old age. They found that garlic could not only stop atherosclerosis in cats, but also reverse it. More precise modern studies over the last twenty years have shown that if rabbits, guinea pigs and other animals are fed cholesterol or butter, together with their normal food, the cholesterol in their blood increases to abnormal levels. But if fresh garlic, garlic juice, garlic oil or other garlic preparations are given as well, the rise is prevented completely. This has been demonstrated in nearly fifty published scientific studies.

For example, in a study at Alcorn State University in Mississippi animals were fed their normal diet, together with cholesterol amounting to 1 per cent of the total foodstuffs (an exceptionally high proportion). Some also received different kinds of dried garlic powder and extract. As expected, the cholesterol levels in blood and liver rose and stayed high. However, the various garlic powders and extracts reduced the cholesterol in the blood by about one quarter, and in the liver by more than one half, back to more or less normal levels.

It was clear that fresh garlic powder and garlic oil were effective. There were several similar studies involving pure allicin and also pure diallyl disulphide, the main ingredient of garlic oil, which showed similar results. These studies showed, therefore, that any odorous preparation of garlic would be effective against atherosclerosis.

It also made little difference whether the increase in fat in the body was produced by feeding the animals butter, lard, cholesterol, a great deal of sugar, or alcohol. All these unusual diets (unusual for the animals, that is!) produced raised levels of cholesterol and blood fat which could be reduced by feeding garlic.

In another example, Professor Bordia, of the Rabindranath Tagore Medical College, Rajasthan, India, who has been a leader in these studies, fed cholesterol-rich food to rabbits and then rather large quantities of garlic oil. He compared the results with those achieved by one of the standard medical treatments given to people with greatly increased cholesterol, namely the drug clofibrate. It turned out that the garlic was more effective than clofibrate at reducing the cholesterol which had accumulated in atherosclerotic plaques. Garlic was also more effective than clofibrate at reducing fatty accumulations in the arteries and blood cholesterol levels.

This research also gives us the opportunity of understanding how garlic achieves this remarkable effect. According to scientists such as David Kritchevsky at the world-famous Wistar Institute in Philadelphia, garlic specifically slows down the manufacture of fats and cholesterol in the liver. It can be shown that it slows down the catalysts, and therefore the whole 'production line' which makes the cholesterol.

This means that levels are reduced even when there is no surplus cholesterol in the diet, a fact which has been demonstrated in several studies on animals. For example, an investigation at the US Department of Agriculture Research Laboratory in Madison, Wisconsin, involved feeding pigs with a normal diet together with garlic extract. The LDL cholesterol, the unwanted type, fell by a half, the HDL increased by 20 per cent and the production of these fats in the liver was halved.

It has been shown that animals fed with garlic excrete more bile as well as fat. Yet another mechanism may therefore be in operation, quite similar to the one used by modern drugs to reduce blood fats. That is, garlic may help the liver to remove the extra cholesterol in the form of bile and then eliminate the bile from the body.

The human experience

One may carry out studies on animals but it is only studies on humans which are really convincing. One point to be made is that animal research always uses exaggeratedly high doses. Will garlic still work on people using normal daily amounts? The various clinical studies carried out have addressed themselves to three main questions. Will garlic help individuals to dispose of extra fat after a fatty meal? Will garlic bring down levels of cholesterol, fats and atherosclerosis in normal people? Will it do so in people already suffering from excessive cholesterol and fat in their body or from heart disease?

In India, where considerable scientific work on garlic has been carried out, there have been studies on the effect of eating garlic and onion at the same time as fats. For example, in a study at the Cardiology Department of Rabindranath Tagore Medical College, Rajasthan, a number of people were given a breakfast which included 100g of butter. This led to a 10 per cent rise in blood cholesterol a few hours afterwards, along with a drop of more than 20 per cent in the fibrinolytic or clot-removing tendency of the blood. However, if garlic juice or garlic oil was taken with the meal, these changes were completely prevented. In fact, the clot-removing tendency was increased by 20 per cent. From this and other similar studies, we can conclude that eating garlic together with fatty food does help people to dispose of fats more easily and reduce their harmful after-effects.

Of course, this should not be taken as licence for an unhealthy diet provided that garlic is taken as an antidote. The risks of atherosclerosis caused by the wrong foods are too great for even garlic to take care of. The logical response to the grossly abnormal cholesterol levels of the majority of Western adults is to stem the tide of fats – that is, to address the root causes of atherosclerosis, and use garlic as an additional aid.

Garlic and raised cholesterol

When garlic is taken in a dose of at least one to two cloves a day (or their equivalent in product form), it will, according to some twenty-five clinical studies, reduce the amount of cholesterol in the blood by an average of 15 per cent, enough to reduce the risk of a heart attack by 30 per cent. For example a study which was completed in 1988 in Germany looked at 40 middle-aged people with high cholesterol levels. Their initial average was 7.6 mmol/l, or 295mg/100ml. Half of the group were given garlic products equivalent to one clove a day for three months. The other half were given a neutral, look-alike preparation. The cholesterol levels of those taking garlic dropped steadily over the three-month period to an average of 6 mmol/l, or 233mg/100ml, a decrease of more than 20 per cent. (Those taking the look-alike remained more or less the same.) This is more than can be expected from regular, modern drugs. In addition, there were no reports of any kind of side-effect. Those taking garlic also felt active and energetic by the end of the period.

The question remains: does garlic reduce cholesterol in everyone, whether they have raised levels or not, or does it only do so in those with problems? The answer is not so clear, since almost everyone in the modern world has levels which are higher than they should be, even the so-called 'normals'. However, it appears from the clinical studies that garlic does have some effect in all cases, but that the more cholesterol there is in the blood in the first place, the more it is reduced. For example, studies in India with people whose cholesterol levels were normal, below 5.2 mmol/l, or 200mg/100ml, found reductions of only a few per cent, while studies of people in the risk area above 6.5 mmol/l, or 250mg/100ml, found a drop of up to a quarter.

Another conclusion to be drawn from the clinical research is that higher doses over longer periods produce better results. Garlic will start to work as soon as it is taken. However, the intake should continue for at least a month for more significant effects to occur.

The evidence also shows that as soon as you stop taking garlic, the level of fat in the blood returns to what it was before. This fact is satisfying to scientists, since it demonstrates that it was the garlic which was having the effect and not something else. To the rest of us it says that garlic is not a magic potion which need only be taken now and again. It is a medicinal food whose regular consumption should be an essential part of fat and cholesterol-lowering life habits.

This reinforcement was well demonstrated in a study by Professor Ernst of the University of Munich, published in the *British Medical Journal*. He chose patients who had high levels of cholesterol (above 6.7 mmol/l, or 260mg/100ml). Half were given a low-calorie diet for four weeks, and half the same diet together with garlic preparation equivalent to just under a clove of garlic a day. Those on the diet had less cholesterol at the end of the period. Those taking garlic as well, even though the dose was modest, achieved a further 10 per cent reduction. This study shows that garlic and general diet should be used to help each other.

It is interesting to see which kind of cholesterol is affected. In the study by Ernst, it was LDL, the unfriendly cholesterol, that was reduced; HDL remained unchanged. Professor Bordia, mentioned above, took 62 patients with heart disease and raised blood cholesterol, and examined the effect of giving them garlic oil and no other types of circulatory medicine. They were compared to a group of healthy people. Over eight months, the healthy people reduced their cholesterol by 15 per cent; their LDL-cholesterol was also reduced by 15 per cent, and their HDL increased by nearly as much. In the group with heart disease, the cholesterol actually increased during the first month and then fell to a 30 per cent lower level by the end of the period. The beneficial changes in LDL and HDL were correspondingly greater than in the normal group.

Professor Bordia suggested that cholesterol may increase in heart patients for a short time after garlic is taken, since the garlic may be dislodging it from the artery walls. If this is true, it would imply that garlic is able to reverse atherosclerosis by removing fatty build-up. It would make garlic curative as well as preventive. The medical dogma used to be that atherosclerosis was a one-way process and could be halted but not reversed. Today it is an open question. Diet and proper treatment can, it seems, reverse it to a greater or lesser extent.

Studies with animals indicate that garlic therapy can actually remove fat from the walls of the blood vessels and that about half the fatty plaques disappear. Two studies used the active ingredients of garlic in pure synthetic form. Scientists from China used pure allicin, and scientists from India used diallyl disulphide, the main ingredients of garlic oil, on atherosclerotic animals. In both cases, they were able to prevent and to some extent remove fatty deposits from the arteries, including the arteries to the heart.

Garlic and the general health of the circulation

It is not easy to assess the health of the human circulatory system other than by measuring the various symptoms of degeneration which occur. The best-known symptom is, of course, the heart attack. However, it would require a long and expensive study to determine whether garlic reduces the number of heart attacks in a given group of people over many years.

It has been shown that garlic reduces a range of other symptoms of atherosclerosis. For a very long time Russian doctors have been using garlic preparations like 'Allifid' as a standard treatment for atherosclerosis, especially in the elderly, and they have reported amelioration of poor circulation in the legs and hands, tiredness and so on.

More recent studies on three hundred patients in Zhenjiang, China, and on a similar number in India, found a rapid improvement in the symptoms of headache, chest pain, tiredness, loss of appetite and digestive problems. However, when the garlic was withdrawn at the end of the study, the symptoms returned. Once more we see garlic's place as a long-term companion to health, not as a short-term remedy.

One relatively common symptom of atherosclerosis is insufficient blood reaching the limbs. As the condition (known as intermittent claudication) becomes worse, it can prevent the sufferer from walking. Garlic has been found to be very helpful in such cases; it enhances the effect of exercise, diet and other treatments, although it works best before the problem has become too severe. A study in Germany, published in the German journal *Medical Practice* in 1986, examined 53 patients before and after four weeks of treatment with doses of garlic equivalent to only a quarter of a clove per day. Tests were carried out on the flow of blood in the legs and it was found to have improved by 50 per cent. Nevertheless, a careful medical analysis of how the symptoms of atherosclerosis are affected by garlic is still awaited.

Garlic and blood pressure

It is natural that if the blood vessels are narrowed by plaques and deposits, the heart will need to pump harder to keep the blood flowing through the many miles of vessels. Atherosclerosis can therefore bring about high blood pressure. This in turn puts an extra load on the heart and can further damage blood vessels, precipitate more atheromas and lead to strokes. High blood pressure is a major cardiac risk factor, rivalling cholesterol. Normal blood pressure is 120 when the heart contracts, 80 when it relaxes, described as 120/80. A 35-year-old man with 150/100 will, according to life insurance statistics, have a 16½ year reduction in life expectancy. Can garlic help?

The answer is that it can, but its effect is mild. Whereas garlic's action on blood fats and, as we shall see in the next chapter, on blood coagulation, is as great as that of regular, modern drugs, this is not the case here.

Until recently, the only evidence available was in medical reports from

Eastern Europe and the USSR, where garlic is part of the regular treatment for high blood pressure. In the last few years, however, several well-conducted medical investigations have been completed in Europe. It was found that a drop of 12-30 millimetres in the upper blood pressure and of 7-20 millimetres in the lower could be obtained by the regular administration of garlic to patients with raised blood pressure. A smaller drop was likely in those with normal blood pressure.

For example, one study, completed in 1988, gave twenty patients tablets equivalent to about half a clove of garlic a day. They were compared to a similar group who received reserpine, a standard drug used to reduce high blood pressure. The study was a double-blind, meaning that neither the patients nor their doctors knew which was which. Within two weeks the average systolic blood pressure (when the heart contracts) in the garlic group dropped from 176 to 164, an average decrease of 7 per cent; the diastolic (when the heart relaxes) came down from 99 to 85, a decrease of 14 per cent. The effect of reserpine was more or less the same. Interestingly, only garlic reduced both blood pressure and blood fat. The drugs used today to treat blood pressure had no effect on cholesterol in the study.

It is clear that fresh garlic, garlic oil and other preparations are all effective. An oil capsule tested on 14 elderly women with high blood pressure brought the less severe cases down to normal. However, those whose condition was due to kidney problems were not affected. In another study on 82 patients, pills of dried garlic were compared to inert, look-alike pills, and blood pressure was reduced within the range already described, while the placebos had almost no effect. In both these studies symptoms such as headache, dizziness, buzzing in the ears and insomnia were considerably improved.

There is an uncertainty about how garlic acts on blood pressure. It used to be thought that it cleaned up putrefying bacteria in the intestine, the kind which change food constituents into various unwanted substances which raise blood pressure. Theories of intestinal hygiene were then at their peak. Today such views are still considered reasonable but have generally been superseded by the evidence that garlic affects the prostaglandins. These substances are present in the blood vessels and are in charge of opening, relaxing or tightening them. If the vessels in the periphery of the body are relaxed, then there is less resistance to the blood flow. So far, there is quite a lot of evidence that garlic increases the flow of blood in the smaller vessels, and we also know that it affects the prostaglandin system. It is therefore reasonable to put the two together. There is also the traditional awareness that garlic makes a person sweat more and so dries out the body; this would also lower blood pressure.

The individual

This chapter has described many studies on human groups. However, the person taking his or her garlic is an individual. Just as the causes and results of circulatory disease differ in each case, so too will garlic's effects. There are indications that for some people it has a very dramatic therapeutic effect, while others do not seem to be greatly improved by it. The overall results, however, are overwhelmingly positive. You should use intelligence and discrimination in selecting any course of treatment and in assessing your personal reactions. In choosing garlic, you will run no risk of adverse effects. It is highly likely that your health will be improved, whether subtly or dramatically. So it is well worth the experiment.

CHAPTER 4

How garlic
thins the blood

————Blood clotting, dietary fat and garlic————

As we have said, blood clots in the arteries are like the pieces which stick to the inside of a kitchen waste pipe. They offer no danger when the blood still flows easily and smoothly through open channels. However, as the vessels are narrowed, this life-saving mechanism operates against our interests. Major clots or thromboses can block the vital coronary arteries and cause a heart attack, or one of the brain blood vessels and cause a stroke, or the vessels in the legs and cause venous thromboses and other problems. The clotting mechanism, and especially the platelets, also play an intimate part in the formation of the atherosclerotic plaques.

Garlic is one of the best anti-clotting remedies that we know. There are several ways in which its effects can be calculated. The strength of the blood's clot-disintegrating mechanism can be measured. So, too, can the tendency of the platelets to clump together or, alternatively, the length of time taken by a sample of the blood to clot. The thinness of the blood, that is to say its fluidity, can also be assessed; this is an important factor in high blood pressure, since the heart has to work harder to push heavier blood around the system.

The amount and quality of dietary fat has a powerful influence on the clotting tendency. Saturated fats and cholesterol increase blood clotting, while at the other end fish oils (and the EPA they contain) reduce it. The initial studies on the effects of garlic tried to find out whether it could remove the increased clotting created in the blood vessels by a fatty meal.

Professor Bordia, one of the pioneers in this field, started investigating garlic as a blood thinner. He was impressed with the ancient Indian wisdom, dating back some two thousand years or more to Charaka, the father of traditional Indian medicine, that garlic helps to maintain the fluidity of the blood, strengthens the heart and prolongs life. 'But for its unpleasant odour,' wrote Charaka, 'garlic would be costlier than gold.' Professor Bordia fed small amounts of cholesterol to rabbits along with their normal diet for several months. The clot-dissipating activity nearly halved over the period because of the increased cholesterol. However, if garlic oil was given along with the fatty diet, not only did the activity not fall, it actually increased by around 10 per cent. In a similar study Professor Bordia found that onion oil could achieve more or less identical effects. These observations have been repeated again and again in laboratories in different parts of the world.

Other, similar studies were also carried out on humans. Again, clot-dissolving activity began to fall after a fatty meal. This could be observed easily and immediately, so it was a relatively simple matter to assess whether garlic could block the effect. Once more it was found that both garlic and onion not only stopped the fall but even increased clot-dissolving activity. One such study was carried out by Professor Menon, then a research fellow at the Royal Victoria Infirmary, Newcastle upon Tyne. His inspiration came, he said, from 'a casual remark by a patient that in France, when a horse develops clots in the legs, it is treated by a diet of garlic and onions'. In a trial 22 patients who were convalescing in his hospital were given a fatty breakfast. After two hours, samples of their blood were taken and the clot-dissolving activity was found to be 25 per cent lower than before eating the meal. However, if they were then given two ounces of fried or boiled onion with the same meal, the activity increased by 50 per cent.

In a similar, more recent study in India, ten healthy people were given a very buttery breakfast and their blood coagulation time was checked. Three hours later this was done again and, as expected, the clot-dissolving activity was down from about 84 units to 43. However, if they took the same breakfast, this time with garlic added to the butter, it went up to 86. Their blood would normally clot in an average of 4 minutes and 15 seconds. After the breakfast it took only 3 minutes, 41 seconds. However, if garlic was added to the butter it took 5 minutes, 7 seconds to clot, slower than normal.

Garlic's effect on blood clotting is indeed dramatic. Its action takes place within a few hours; it is easy to measure, and it is major. Unlike cholesterol levels, which are quite hard to change, ingestion of garlic leads to large and immediate reductions in the clotting tendency. This is partly due to the effectiveness of garlic and partly due to the fact that clotting generally responds more easily to changes in diet and other factors; a good bout of exercise will also produce a quite obvious reduction.

It is clear that garlic increases fibrinolytic (clot-dispersing) activity and reduces clotting times both in normal people and in those suffering from heart disease or atherosclerosis. For example, a study published in 1981 in the specialist journal *Atherosclerosis* involved 20 subjects who all had coronary heart disease. They had all had previous heart attacks. Their clot-dissolving activity started in the morning at 62 units and rose slightly during the day to 70 units. However, if they were given either fried or raw garlic, the activity increased within six hours to over 100 units. When they were given garlic for one month continuously, it went up even higher, to 122 units with fresh garlic and 110 with fried. The garlic was stopped at that point and within two weeks the activity was back to the original level.

An analysis of 15 similar clinical studies involving hundreds of subjects shows garlic increasing the clot-dispersing ability of the blood by an average of 60 per cent. This could be achieved after taking garlic for one day, although the effects did also tend to increase with time. When the garlic was removed from the diet, it gradually fell back to what it was before. In this case fresh and fried garlic were found to work more or less equally well. Other reports confirm that garlic oil, garlic extract, fresh or dried garlic, and onion or onion oil were all similarly effective at thinning the blood.

All these observations were so remarkable and well-defined that in 1981 *The Lancet*, the world's most prestigious medical journal, announced in an enthusiastic editorial that it had high hopes for a natural reduction in blood clotting by dietary factors such as garlic.

As is clear from the research described above, onion can also effect the clotting process, perhaps almost as strongly as garlic. However, onion cannot replace garlic as a treatment for the heart, as it does not have its other effects, such as lowering the levels of fats and cholesterol; it is not such a good, all-round remedy.

Garlic, platelets and the stickiness of the blood

Platelets are the small cell fragments which are the advance guard of the clotting process. They are acutely sensitive to disturbances and chemical triggers which might indicate a wound or break. A variety of influences are known to make them clump or stick together; these include the presence in the blood of the protein fibres which are normally part of the tissues and should not be present in the blood vessels unless there is some kind of fracture. That well-known alarm bell, adrenalin, will also cause the platelets to clump, a mechanism obviously intended to prepare the body for possible injury.

The speed at which the platelets clump together is a very sensitive indicator of how sticky the blood is, how soon it will clot, and the likelihood of the clotting occurring where it is not wanted – that is, in the atherosclerotic blood vessels themselves. Atherosclerosis is always accompanied by some increase in blood stickiness. The speed of clumping is also the easiest, most reliable and quickest of all tests of the effectiveness of garlic. One only has to give a person garlic to eat, wait a short while, and take a little blood. Then it is a simple matter to check under a microscope how fast the platelets clump when triggered to do so by, for example, adrenalin.

Such tests have been carried out by many scientists. These include Dr David Bouillin, who was working as a member of a Medical Research Council team in Oxford, UK. He found that the prevention of clumping is noticeable within an hour after garlic is eaten and that it continues for three to four hours, after which the clumping returns to normal. This gives us a clear picture of how garlic enters the body, acts therapeutically, and is then removed in the same way as other foods or medicines.

It is interesting that the doses of garlic needed to reduce platelet clumping significantly are low. A clear effect on the platelets can be achieved with doses of less than half a clove. If this restricts blood clotting for a few hours, then one clove per day, or its equivalent in product form, divided into two doses, morning and evening, would be the safe minimum necessary to generate scentifically noticeable effects on the body. Again, there is little doubt that fresh garlic, extracts and garlic oil are all effective.

Indeed, patients with high blood cholesterol have been given only one quarter of a clove of garlic per day for three months and the stickiness and clumping tendency measured. Gradually, over the period, the clumping tendency was reduced by 20 per cent and the stickiness by around 30 per cent.

Because this method is such a simple and sensitive barometer of garlic's effects on the body, it has attracted a considerable world research effort. The goal has been to identify which compounds within garlic affect the platelet system and also to determine how they achieve it. In each

Table 1

Research Team	Compounds Discovered	Comment
Dept of Biochemistry, George Washington University School of Medicine, Washington, DC	Adenosine Allicin Dimethyl Trisulphide (and related poly-sulphides)	Present in fresh garlic juice, extract, etc.
Dept of Pathology, College of Medicine, University of Utah	Allicin	as above
Institute of Pharmaceutical Biology, University of Munich, Munich	Ajoene Vinyl 1-2, dithiin Diallyl disulphide	Not in fresh garlic. May be in fried garlic
Dept of Physiology, Nikon University School of Medicine, Tokyo	Methyl Allyl Trisulphide (MATS)	Present at around 5% in garlic oil
Dept of Chemistry, University of Delaware, USA	Diallyl Trisulphide Vinyl 1-2, dithiin 1,5,hexadienyl-trisulphide	Not in fresh garlic. May be in fried garlic
Department of Chemistry, State University of New York, Albany	Ajoene	As above
University of Cologne, Germany	Adenosine	As above

case, scientists have broken down and refined garlic into its component parts and have tested each for blood clotting effects. Finally they have arrived at the single pure compound which they consider the most effective. Unfortunately, though many teams have expended a great deal of effort, they have all arrived at different conclusions.

The results are summarized in the table above. At present we do not know which of these compounds are the most effective. It is only safe to say that each is highly active. The effect of whole garlic and its products is likely to be that of the sum of all the active constituents which it contains. However, how much there is of each of the compounds in different kinds of garlic or garlic products is hard to say.

It is interesting to note that at least two of these compounds, 'Ajoene' and methyl allyl trisulphide ('MATS') are now undergoing tests as possible pure and safe pharmaceuticals against blood clotting.

A great deal of knowledge has now accumulated concerning how garlic and the above constituents work in preventing blood clotting. It is generally agreed that the sulphur compounds interfere with the chemical machinery making the prostaglandins which control the way platelets clump. It is interesting that aspirin, the remedy often given by doctors to prevent blood clotting, works in a similar manner. Incidentally, comparative trials of aspirin and garlic show that, at recommended doses, garlic has at least as much effect on blood clotting.

Garlic influences the prostaglandins in the walls of the blood vessels as well as in the platelets themselves. It increases the production of prostacyclin, which limits clotting, and reduces that of thromboxane A_2, which encourages it.

There may be concern that blood clotting is an essential process which should not be interfered with. However, this is unfounded, since the clotting tendency of people in modern, developed countries is already too high. Garlic simply lowers it to a more normal level. Moreover, there is no evidence that people who eat a very large amount of garlic in their daily diet have a problem with too much bleeding. In various studies people have been given the equivalent of two heads of garlic a day (about twenty cloves) for months, without noticing any tendency to bleed excessively.

However, it would be as well to note that if garlic is being taken along with aspirin and anti-coagulant drugs, the effects can reinforce each other. This will not normally be harmful but should perhaps be avoided in special situations such as surgery.

CHAPTER 5

Garlic and the overall care of your heart

The potential of garlic

Garlic has a unique position in the fight against heart disease, a position held by virtually no other remedy. Its advantages can be summarized as follows:

1. It works simultaneously on several levels

Garlic can significantly lower cholesterol and the overall level of fats in the blood; it is probably as effective as the drugs which are usually used to lower cholesterol levels. At the same time, it has a mild blood pressure-lowering effect. Thirdly, it thins the blood and prevents clotting or thromboses in the blood vessels. Therefore, it protects the heart and circulation against the three main causes of atherosclerosis and heart attacks. There are no conventional drugs which act simultaneously at these three critical points. Cholesterol-lowering drugs such as clofibrate or gem-fibrazole reduce cholesterol and fats and do have some anticlotting effect but do not affect blood pressure. There are blood pressure-lowering drugs (such as diuretics or beta-blockers) which do not affect cholesterol or blood clotting, and there are mild anti-clotting remedies (such as aspirin), which do not have the other effects.

2. Garlic is safe

All drugs (and even, on occasions, medicinal foods) have side-effects. In the case of garlic, however, they are so minimal that the German Federal Health Board declared it to have 'No known side-effects'. A few people do have reactions to fresh garlic – either allergic reactions on the skin while cutting it, or digestive reactions such as nausea and repeating: however, these effects do not last long. Modern garlic products are very unlikely to cause these reactions. On the other hand, the drugs used in the management of coronary heart disease, angina, very high cholesterol levels and other indications of atherosclerosis, certainly do have side-effects. In the case of the blood pressure drugs, for example, these range from mild gastric disturbances and mild depression, to asthma or impotence. Garlic is a harmless medicinal food consumed daily by a good proportion of the inhabitants of our globe. It has been eaten for thousands of years without harm and with a good deal of benefit. It has, indeed, an astonishing track record for safety.

3. Garlic is a true preventive remedy
Garlic can be taken for life without the alarming feeling that you have become tied to drugs for the rest of your life. It is a natural remedy which can be incorporated easily into any self-care regimen. It is the ideal aid if the signs of atherosclerosis are still mild, merely the first hint of trouble. If your cholesterol levels, for example, are in the grey area above 5.2 mmol/l, or 200mg/100ml but below 6.5 mmol/l, or 250mg/100ml, or if your blood pressure is around 150, your medical advisor will be reluctant to start prescribing drugs. These are reserved for more serious cases. Often he or she will do nothing, or very little - a mention of saturated fat, an admonishment about smoking, an encouragement to exercise and a short sermon on peace of mind. Modern medicine is strong on curative prescription but weak on preventive instruction. Yet something must be done to halt the heart disease epidemic. This is where garlic comes into its own - in the intermediate area where prevention is necessary but treatment is not.

4. Garlic can be a pleasure
Garlic is more than just a medicine - its flavour forms a key part of the world's cuisine. For those who are attuned to it, it provides a considerable enrichment of the table. Those who are not can begin by taking capsules or tablets, and may come to appreciate it in time. It fits perfectly into the kind of diet which, as we describe below, will help to prevent cardiovascular problems.

──Garlic as a part of preventive heart care──
Garlic may be useful, but it cannot purge the world of its major health problems unaided. It is not a panacea. Those who really know how to use it regard garlic as an important dietary tool which should take its

place in the self-care tool-kit along with all the other aids that nature has been thoughtful enough to provide. Garlic cannot be expected to provide the whole answer after the damage has been done. Indeed, this would be treating it just like a modern drug, and it is drug-dependent attitudes which have to some extent created the problems of heart disease in the first place. These say that it does not really matter what you do or how you live, because there will always be a pill available to put you right.

It is unlikely that garlic alone will bring the risk of heart disease down to that of vegetarians or Japanese people following a traditional diet. However, its use as part of an overall self-care regimen should be able to achieve this. Moreover, it is not only the health of the arteries that will be improved. Just as garlic itself has a range of benefits, so too will the principles of health care which we are about to outline. Common problems such as tiredness, headaches, obesity, colitis, arthritis, Candida, hypoglycaemia, cancer and lowered immunity can all be prevented and often actually cured in this way.

Some may react against what they see as an obsessive concern with health matters, just as there are those who dislike the idea of garlic. This is largely a cultural problem. The traditional, well-tried methods of maintaining health, which are part of our national heritages, have been largely lost. Gone too, at least in Northern Europe and America, has been the automatic use of garlic and other medicinal foods. To re-establish their use in your personal life may require a little more effort, a rather more special interest. But the principles of self-care are coming back. Even government agencies encourage it more than they did ten years ago. Eventually garlic and the other medicinal foods will make a full return to popularity and then it will be easier for all of us.

———Towards a programme for prevention———

'Stop in the name of love, before you break my heart,' goes the well-known song. The first way to protect the circulation, and therefore the heart, is simply to stop abusing it. Modern life presents us with a constant succession of interconnected influences which weigh on our vascular systems. Indeed, we regard high blood pressure and heart attacks as more or less inevitable for adult males, much like tuberculosis in the last century or malaria in the tropics. Yet the Japanese do not suffer from atherosclerosis (that is, unless they emigrate to a western country). They eat less than a third of the fat the Westerners eat, and the traditional Japanese diet has no dairy products, meat products, sugar, bread or cakes, although this is of course now changing.

The blood pressure of the Solomon Islanders, the Aborigines and other such races goes down with age, not up. They eat no salt. The Eskimos eat a great deal of fat, and live without heart problems; however, they are protected by fish oil and they too eat no salt or dairy products.

From very extensive reviews of who is, and who is not, vulnerable to heart disease, we learn of the role of smoking; of the dangers of stress, anxiety and tension; of the essential need for exercise; of the need for vitamins, essential fatty acids, fibre and other food factors; and of the subsidiary risks of coffee, pesticides and the like. The importance of all of these factors has been confirmed by extensive work in the laboratory.

It is interesting that this entire research effort is steadily drawing us towards conclusions reached long ago by Hippocrates, Galen, the ancient Egyptian physicians and the preventive advice given by naturopathy, herbalism and traditional Chinese and Indian medicine. They have always emphasized the necessity for moderation ('man lives on one quarter of what he eats, the doctors live on the rest', goes an ancient saying), a wholesome diet, exercise and a sanguine approach to life. Among the specific remedies of ancient times, garlic figures prominently.

Here are the main items to consider in relation to cardiovascular health. You will know which is most relevant to you.

--------------------- Diet ---------------------

Doctors are now unanimous in recommending a reduction in saturated fats. A leaflet issued in 1985 by the UK Department of Health, for example, advised a drop in fatty meats and full-fat dairy products, so reducing fat intake from 40 per cent of the diet to one-third. More consumption of fruits, vegetables and fibre-containing foods was recommended. This is a start, but from a medical point of view it is certainly not strong enough. If followed, it will achieve a mere 10–20 per cent drop in heart disease. A proper consideration of the risks could only conclude that, in order to achieve a substantial reduction, it is absolutely necessary to disrupt established eating habits. If, to take the extreme case, the whole population of Britain were to turn vegetarian, cholesterol levels would be reduced by 25 per cent, the blood clotting tendency would fall considerably, blood pressure would come down to normal and deaths from heart attacks would take place at 40 per cent of the present level.

Here are some guidelines for a diet that really will make a difference:

Carbohydrates

Carbohydrates include all the sweet or starchy, energy-giving food substances contained in potatoes, bread, pasta, rice and other grains, and sugar-containing foods. They are the mainstay of your diet and they should make up two-thirds of everything you eat. From the heart's point of view, all carbohydrates are perfectly satisfactory provided they are not refined or 'empty'. Natural carbohydrates have 10 per cent of their weight as fibre, vitamins, essential minerals and fats, and can be eaten freely unless you are actually obese. When refined, however, they present problems for the body.

Carbohydrate cautions

● Avoid white flour in bread, cakes, biscuits, puddings etc. It deprives you of valuable fibre and vitamins. As it is too easily transformed into sugars in the digestive system, it puts a strain on the pancreas, which has to dispose of the sudden surge. It is soon converted into fat anyway.
● Avoid sweets, chocolates, cakes, custard, puddings, etc. These also add 'empty' carbohydrates which lead to higher amounts of fat in the blood.

Positive carbohydrate sources

● Use whole wheat bread, whole wheat pasta and foods made with whole wheat flour. Oats, barley, maize, buckwheat, rye, millet, brown rice, tapioca, and semolina are sources of carbohydrates which, if unrefined, can be the basis of multitudes of dishes, either as whole grains, flakes or flours.
● Lentils, pulses and nuts contain a great deal of beneficial carbohydrates.
● If you have a sweet tooth, eat dried fruit, molasses or a little honey or brown sugar.

Garlic goes well with pickles, sauces, and dips for use with wholemeal bread. A classical Middle Eastern dip which is excellent for health consists of olive oil, lemon, garlic and hyssop (a relative of oregano). In the Mediterranean, garlic is used in country bread and pasta sauces, and fried in risottos and rice dishes.

Protein

Protein provides the essential 'building blocks' for the body. However, it should be in second place to carbohydrates in the diet. An average Western adult eats too much protein, to which the body then adapts; you can gradually adjust to eating less, to your benefit.

Types of protein to reduce

● Eat less meat. Try to avoid fatty meat, hamburgers, hot dogs, sausages, pork and bacon altogether. Eat meat sparingly. Don't eat meat pies, chicken pies or processed forms of meat products.
● Avoid eggs. One a day is too many, especially if they come from conventional farms. Try to buy free-range eggs if you can: they are better for your health and taste better too.
● Avoid full-fat cheeses, such as Cheddar, Stilton and cream cheese. Try to eat less cheese altogether and, if necessary, use curd cheese, Greek sheep's cheese or cottage cheese.
● Avoid cow's milk; adults don't need it.

Positive protein sources

● If you eat meat, make sure that it is as lean as possible.
● Use vegetarian pies or spreads instead of meat.
● Eat more fish, especially mackerel, herring, tuna, sardines and salmon, which are rich in fish-oil.
● Try tofu and soya milk instead of cow's milk.
● The mainstay of vegetarian protein sources are pulses and seeds. Sesame seeds have more protein per unit weight than meat. Try to eat a continuously changing variety of pulses and seeds. These include split peas, lentils, lima beans, broad beans, chickpeas, humus, tehina, soya beans, sunflower seeds, mung beans and the 'macrobiotic meat', aduki beans.

Garlic goes well with lean meat, especially in French garlic sauces. Both garlic and rosemary are healthy additions to roasts. Garlic also goes well with fish. You can add crushed garlic and dill to curd cheese to give it a rich, aromatic flavour. Crushed garlic is a necessary addition to humus, tehina and cooked soya beans. Add a little garlic and yeast extract to nut roasts, casseroles and lentil pies.

Fats

Fats are the major present-day problem for the circulation. Try to reduce fat to no more than 15 per cent of your diet. This means frying food rarely and never deep-frying, and drastically reducing the fatty sources of protein, particularly dairy products and meat.

Reducing fats

● Avoid saturated fats as much as possible. As we have seen, reduce consumption of animal products, including dairy products. Always use oil, never butter, for cooking and frying.
● Choose a vegetable oil-based, unsaturated margarine for spreading on bread instead of butter, and spread thinly.

Positive fat facts

● The best oils for cooking are cold-pressed, first pressed or virgin vegetable oils. This means that they are pressed in the traditional way without refining. It doesn't matter so much which oil it is – soya, sunflower, corn, safflower – what matters is that it should be unrefined. Refining drastically reduces the quantity of beneficial and necessary oils by converting them into unnecessary oils. Cold-pressed oils are not widely available, so look for them in health stores.
● For spreading, use margarine based on the above, cold-pressed, oils if possible. This should also be available in health food shops. Use vegetable oil instead of margarine wherever possible in pastry. Consider other spreads such as tofu, tehina, nut butters and vegetable spreads as alternatives to margarine.
● Use cold-pressed, virgin olive oil wherever possible (e.g. in salads), although it is not the best oil for cooking.

Garlic is fried in oil, often with onion, in Indian and Chinese cooking and in other ethnic dishes. The oil is then used as the basis for numerous dishes such as curries. Virgin olive oil, together with lemon, cider vinegar, garlic, and a little mustard and herbs, is the best basic salad dressing.

Fibre, vitamins and minerals

Fibre refers to all the indigestible material contained in vegetable sources of food. It provides the bulk, or 'roughage', that the digestive system requires to work properly. Lack of fibre in the diet is a modern phenomenon, since food refining and processing removes it. Soluble fibre, found in oats, fruit and vegetables, is especially important to those at risk from heart disease because it binds fats and cholesterol and removes them from the body. (The modern cholesterol-lowering drugs are also based on the constituents of food fibre.)

Positive, natural sources

● There should be around 40g of fibre in the diet per day. Leafy vegetables contain 5–9g of fibre in every 100g, wholewheat flour 9g. The main source of vitamins and minerals, as well as some necessary fats and other dietary constituents, is vegetables. Vegetables and salads should be regarded as an essential part of the diet, not as decorative accessories. There should be one vegetable-based meal every day, otherwise it will be hard to obtain the necessary nutrients.

● Vegetables should be as fresh as possible. A sodden mass of over-cooked cabbage is not going to give you much, nor is a tin of coloured green peas or launderetted baby carrots. The best vegetables are organically grown, fresh vegetables in salad. If you can't find them, at least buy the freshest vegetables you can. However, don't undo all the good of your salads with lashings of mayonnaise. Vegetables like spinach should be cooked very lightly, by boiling, steaming, or braising for the minimum time.

● It is unnecessary, and expensive, to take tablets made of fibre or to pour bran on your foods. If your diet contains a sufficient daily intake of vegetables, salads, whole grains and fruit, it will not be necessary to add extra fibre. Moreover, poor quality, empty, refined foods cannot be fully restored by adding fibre and vitamins. Many other nutrients will still be missing.

Garlic is a rich source of minerals and also contains trace elements such as germanium and selenium.

Salt

Since it raises blood pressure, salt is one of the major risk factors in heart disease. It has now been demonstrated conclusively that it is unnecessary on health grounds to add any salt to the diet. It used to be held that the body needs salt to make up its losses on sweating. However, scientists have now found that the body actually needs very little salt, and there is enough in the diet already without additions. Sweating only removes excess salt. In hot countries those people who don't eat salt sweat pure water; those that do eat salt, sweat salt. You would be well-advised to reduce salt in the diet. Fortunately, there is a range of salt-substitutes available, including and especially potassium salt. Spices and herbs often provide a healthy and flavourful substitute.

Garlic provides a rich rather than a salty flavour. However, mixing it with other herbs such as parsley and basil produces such an interesting aroma that the addition of salt becomes less relevant.

Drink

● **Coffee** is not particularly helpful to the heart and if possible should be reduced. Two and a half cups will double the level of adrenalin circulating. It also makes the heart itself more sensitive to the damage caused by the adrenalin excess. In others words, coffee and stress together are an unwholesome combination. Coffee made from grains, dandelion or chicory, or decaffeinated coffee, can be convenient instant substitutes.

● **Tea** is also caffeinated, though it has tannins which are known to help remove fats in the digestive system. The current enthusiasm for herb teas greatly increases the range of hot drinks available.

● **Alcohol** is chemically from the same family as fat, so the same rules apply to both. However, a little wine is said to be beneficial to the heart.

Some suggestions on changing your diet

The major difficulty in improving your diet is to break old habits. Unfortunately, many people only summon the will to change after some obvious symptom of heart disease occurs and the driving force is then fear. It is much better to act before trouble develops. Nevertheless, it is never too late to make an improvement.

The change can be made in various ways. The bold souls make a clean break: a period in a health resort, or a visit to a naturopath with a diet sheet to take home, or a supervised period of fasting and a complete clean-up, can be an excellent way to start. It will make you feel good; a multitude of small symptoms disappear and general vitality is restored, and this provides the motivation to continue.

Another way is to change the diet gradually, by substitution. That is, keep the same dietary patterns but change the items: brown bread for white, oil for butter, fish for meat, rice for chips and so on. You can move imperceptibly towards a wholefood diet without noticing it.

A key element is to be in touch with your food. That is, regard it as important, interesting and a source of pleasure. One of the risks of giving health advice, as in these pages, is that it may produce a sense of guilt and aversion towards what you eat and an unwilling struggle to improve - like the Victorian schoolboy forced to eat a mountain of mashed potato. The answer is to be aware of what you eat and explore new foods with a sense of experiment and adventure. Make them pleasant to look at and taste, and involve friends and family in the proceedings. One interesting way of doing this is to cook foreign foods - Chinese, Indian, Japanese, Greek, or Mexican food often contain the healthy constituents we have been discussing.

Another common pitfall is to pay too much attention to advertisements. The end result is a substitution of one set of packaged, instant, processed foods for another. It is a common reflex in our modern world to respond to all changes required of us by buying something. In the case of food, it is helpful to become less of a purchaser and more of a preparer. Deal more with real foods - grains, vegetables, pulses, fresh fish - and less with those that have been pre-prepared.

We have left to last what is perhaps most important of all: children. Heart attacks at 40 have their origins in the eating habits established in childhood. Children will generally like the food common to the society around them; responding to the world's blandishments, they will be drawn to a diet of sweet, packaged and processed foods. At home, however, they should receive only real, nutritious foods. Parents who say: 'I've tried them with vegetables, they won't eat them,' reveal resignation and their own basic lack of interest. Try getting your children to share in the adventure of discovering real food. If you are consistent and imaginative about this, they will like and ask for wholefood and regard junk foods as suspect.

Special foods that help the heart

All the *alliums* besides garlic are helpful. Onions, for example, have similar, though weaker, effects on the circulation. Chives and leeks should not be ignored. Of the other vegetables, radishes and the brassicas, especially cauliflower and Brussels sprouts, are useful in detoxifying the liver.

The minerals magnesium, potassium and manganese are of special importance to the heart and circulation. These can be found in seeds such as sesame and sunflower seeds, in molasses, dark green leafy vegetables like spinach, parsley, and apple juice or cider vinegar, all of which are highly recommended.

Spices and herbs can be very helpful. For example, ginger stimulates and calms the digestion, and also reduces cholesterol in the blood. All pungent spices, including ginger, cloves, horseradish and mustard, open the peripheral blood vessels, encourage sweating and, in moderation, can be helpful to the circulation. Herbs such as rosemary, thyme, bay, mint and sage all have useful medicinal effects. For example, they are anti-infective, they are antioxidants which preserve beneficial body fats, and they help against stomach and intestinal problems.

The need for exercise

Proper exercise is one of the most important keys to a healthy heart. It is advisable to exercise vigorously at least one a day. Traditionally, exercise is described as vigorous if it makes you sweat. The amount of exercise is very much dependent on how fit you are. If you are not fit, you should build up to it very gradually.

Exercise is more beneficial if it is regular and rhythmic – swimming, jogging, dancing, skiing, digging, cycling, yoga or T'ai chi are all excellent forms of exercise. The body does better on less intense exercise for a longer time than very intense exercise for a short period, followed by inactivity.

Likewise, exercise should be kept up as far as possible throughout life. There are many stories of keen sportsmen whose first heart attack happened after they gave up all sports and went to fat in their middle age. It would have been better to have done less but to have kept it going more regularly.

The benefits of exercise are well known. The levels of cholesterol are substantially decreased. The clot-removing activity of the blood is increased and clots are less likely to form because the blood is thinner and flows faster. Arteries expand, offering less resistance, blood pressure falls, stress is dissipated, the heart becomes slower and stronger, and there is some evidence of a reversal of atherosclerotic plaques in the arteries. The list could continue. A range of studies have concluded that regular exercise reduces the risk of a heart attack by at least half.

The need for calm

Stress can damage the circulation, whether dietary or other factors are working for or against it. In fact, the discovery of the effects of stress arose through a study which tried to determine why some people with a great deal of furring of the arteries succumbed to heart trouble while others were free of it. The answer lay in the different ways in which the people reacted to the challenges of life.

Those people, especially men, who are irritable, anxious, constantly over-stimulated, under strain, perfectionist, tense, clock-watching, ambitious, impatient or angry all suffer from too much physiological arousal. Their adrenalin is constantly circulating, their stress hormones are erratic, and the result is narrowed arteries, higher blood pressure, heart damage and twice the risk of heart disease. Other diseases are also increased as stress reduces the body's immunity. Surveys have found that two out of three visits to general practitioners in modern cities are made for stress-related conditions. The natural systems which make us alert when faced with danger have themselves become dangerous by responding so relentlessly to the challenges and disturbances of modern life.

There are several answers to this problem. Cardiologists like Professor Peter Nixon at Charing Cross Hospital, London, now teach relaxation and counselling to cardiac patients as a frontline defence against internal alarm systems. It has been found that if the adrenalin can sometimes be switched off completely, it is able to function in a less damaging manner. Researchers at St George's Hospital Medical School and other hospitals have found that regular deep relaxation sessions will reduce blood pressure by 15–20 per cent and cholesterol levels by 10 per cent.

Relaxation training is easily undertaken. It is taught in many parts of the world at health centres and in private groups and can even be done from tapes. The states produced are akin to the deep peace felt when quietly absorbed in pleasant daydreams or a beautiful piece of music. Once you learn how to relax deeply, the memory of the state will be with you as a permanent assistance in stressful moments.

Sometimes relaxation training can be helped by biofeedback. This involves using a small monitor by which you can check on your level of relaxation and so guide yourself deeper.

Counselling is also very useful. Post-heart attack patients are often brought together in guided groups in order to discuss their problems. The support offered by such groups is known to help prevent recurrences. Counselling ranges from the provision of a good listener to whom one can unburden oneself, all the way to psychotherapy. It has become common practice for large corporations to have a free counselling service available to executives so as to reduce the build-up of stress.

A more profound method of mental control is meditation, of which there are many different techniques. Here the relaxation is deepened so as to enter states of quiet watchfulness. One modern version, sometimes called autogenic training, employs the use of affirmative statements about the health of the body and the circulation. These act much like hypnosis in releasing interior tensions and improving bodily states. There is considerable evidence of the positive physiological effects of meditation practices on the circulation and the blood. Moreover, these methods are very helpful in giving you more control over your lifestyle and habits.

Smoking

Smokers have a much higher risk of heart disease. This is partly because nicotine constricts the blood vessels, especially the coronary arteries. The carbon monoxide from the burning tobacco also puts a strain on the heart. Nicotine is probably the most widely used toxin in our society and giving up smoking is not easy. There is, nevertheless, a steady social move away from it, which should be helpful. Probably the best thing to do is to spend as much time as possible with non-smokers. Try to add other things to your life to take its place – extra exercise or nibbling some nuts and raisins. Most people put on weight after giving up cigarettes, but this can be dealt with when it happens.

Other herbs and supplements for the circulation

Though garlic is uniquely effective as a daily preventive remedy for the circulation, there are other herbs and food supplements that are of interest.

Fish oil, containing EPA

EPA is a fat that is made by the human body in small amounts from essential dietary fats. It is a starting material for the manufacture of certain substances which, as we saw in chapter 4, influence clotting and local constriction of the vessels. It has been found that EPA changes the balance of these substances so as to reduce platelet clumping, increase clotting time and improve the blood's fat content.

The value of EPA was discovered by examining the diet of Eskimos who, despite consuming a great deal of fat, have low levels of heart disease. Fish oil together with its EPA was found to be the answer and, as a result of many laboratory and clinical studies around the world, this is now accepted as a medicine by health authorities. Besides being available on chemists' shelves, it is also given as a prescription for patients with heart disease. The clinical studies have almost all been done on the main fish oil product, which is called MaxEPA. This has been shown to ameliorate angina and peripheral vascular disease. It lowers the levels of cholesterol and blood fat, especially that of one of the main carriers of cholesterol, Very Low Density Lipoprotein. It also reduces clotting and stickiness.

Fish oils are a nutritional supplement which, in the long-term will gradually adjust the fat content in the tissues. Garlic is more medicinal and works more immediately than EPA, although its effects wear off more quickly when it is not taken. Garlic seems to reduce cholesterol and LDL more markedly than EPA but to have a different effect on the clotting process. Garlic and EPA therefore make good partners, complementing each other by working rather differently against the build-up of atherosclerosis.

Magnesium

This is the mineral most closely linked to heart problems. Many experts regard a lack of magnesium in the diet as producing heart damage, sensitivity of the heart to attack by stress hormones and problems with heart rhythm. A lack of magnesium may be a cause of sudden death in people with heart disease. It can protect the heart during and after a heart attack. It would be wise to take supplements such as dolomite if there is a magnesium deficiency in the diet. The recommended level is 300mg a day, and a processed food diet may contain only a fraction of this.

Dark green vegetables, nuts, seeds, wholemeal flour and molasses are all rich in magnesium. The presence of magnesium in the water supply may be the reason for the lower levels of heart disease in areas which have hard water compared to those with soft.

Vitamin E

Vitamin E is a somewhat mysterious fatty vitamin. Together with vitamin C and selenium, it is part of the body's anti-oxidation system. This ensures that the body fats keep in good shape and do not become rancid; it helps to protect the walls of the arteries and the cells of the blood. For that reason, vitamin E can be used to treat diseases of the peripheral circulation, for example in the legs or the eyes. It helps to move oxygen around the body and can therefore bring extra amounts to the heart and protect it from damage during atherosclerosis. However, since sudden, large doses can raise blood pressure, it is best to take vitamin E under the guidance of a medical or nutritional expert. Small amounts of vitamin E are available in wheat germ (which you should store in the fridge) and in whole grains.

Rutin

Rutin is a material that is found in the flowers and leaves of buckwheat. It protects fragile blood vessels. For that reason, it is used to prevent damage to the small blood vessels and as a treatment of varicose veins.

Herbal teas

Two widely available, tasty herbal teas can help to lower blood pressure. They are lime flower tea and hibiscus flower tea.

─────── Herbal medicines for the heart ───────

There are a range of herbal medicines which are used to treat heart conditions, either as a replacement for, or in addition to, conventional medical treatment. The herbalist can often provide mixtures which are effective in an early stage of heart disease when the use of conventional drugs is rejected because of side-effects. All these herbs should be used under professional guidance for proper effect. Possibilities include:

● **Hawthorn** (Crataegus oxyacantha). The flowers and leaves provide one of the main remedies for the heart, stimulating circulation in the coronary vessels and protecting and supporting the heart muscle in old age and heart disease.

● **Ginkyo biloba** is an ancient Oriental remedy which has recently been rediscovered. It opens the arteries and therefore helps the peripheral circulation (e.g. the legs) and the circulation in the brain.

● **Mistletoe** (Viscum album) can be used for high blood pressure and is effective over long periods. It helps with symptoms such as dizziness. However, it should be used only under professional guidance.

● **Butcher's broom** (Ruscus aculeatus) root is used to restore circulation in the veins rather than the arteries. It is used to treat varicose veins and is a diuretic, removing excess water from the body. The flowers of broom have a special heart-supporting effect. They regulate the beat of the heart and help prevent disturbances of heart rhythm.

● **Lily of the Valley** (Convallaria majalis) is a heart stimulant and will help to support a weak heart.

────── Daily heart care - an overview ──────

We have looked at a number of aspects of our daily lives. Poor diet, too much salt, smoking, lack of exercise, stress and toxins have been identified scientifically as the main causes of atherosclerosis and heart disease. Garlic, EPA, magnesium, fibre and herbs offer positive protection. But how are we to remember all this advice? It must, at times, seem complex enough to make us throw up our hands in the air, have a good steak, and say: 'To hell with health!'

The answer is to keep recalling the reason why there is an epidemic of heart disease. Remember that it is a new event. Our ancestors were not affected by it. Nor are the so-called primitive peoples, the Aborigines, the Bedouin, the Zulus, the Eskimos, even if they eat meat and smoke – unless, that is, they join modern society, when they succumb like the rest of us. Animals, too, don't suffer from heart disease unless we experimentally feed them our own diets.

The main reason for the epidemic is that the modern world has relentlessly substituted synthetic products and materials for the real thing. Wild animals grazing on wild plants produce meat that contains EPA and a minimum of saturated fat. Vegetables and whole grains have always been full of minerals and necessary nutrients. We have processed them mercilessly; 'Long Shelf Life Equals Short Human Life' is a well-known slogan. Exercise was once a natural part of daily life. Now we are obliged to sit around all week and confine ourselves to unhealthy bursts carried out, if at all, on Saturdays. Stress used to be reserved for special events. Now it is relaxation which is special. Garlic and other medicines used to be everyday foods, built into the diet through the natural wisdom of society. Now we have to write books about their health benefits in order to persuade people to go back to them.

The logic of the do's and don'ts is to keep as much as possible to the simpler and more tangible aspects of life. When in doubt, select the more unrefined, the more substantial, the less artificial. It may not be so convenient to cook fresh vegetables. But then neither is a heart attack convenient.

There is another essential guide and that is yourself. You may not feel atherosclerosis creeping up. But if you do take care of yourself in the ways outlined above, you will feel better, more positive, more energetic and with fewer petty symptoms. Exercise will make you feel good. Vegetarian food will make you feel lighter. Relaxation will help you perform better.

─────────────────**Case histories**─────────────────

Consider, for example, the case of James W., a legal officer in an inner city local authority. He was married, 51 years old and regarded himself as reasonably fit. However, he was frequently off work with colds and catarrh and he quite often felt depressed. One day, while climbing a hill in his local park, he had acute chest pains. It was like someone sitting on his chest. His doctor diagnosed angina and found his cholesterol to be near 7.8 mmol/l, or 300mg/100ml, and his blood pressure a little above normal. He gave him something to take whenever he had an attack, pills against cholesterol, and fish oil, and advised him to change his diet, which was traditional. It turned out that he used to be a keen tennis player but now only watched it on the TV. His doctor advised him to take it up again in stages. However, the attacks continued and he felt even more depressed at how difficult it was to change his habits and how far away he was from returning to real physical activity.

Eventually he went to a naturopath, who prescribed a strict diet, vitamin tablets, hawthorn as a daily tincture and garlic capsules morning and evening. He began to lose weight immediately and with every ounce some of his depression and sense of failure disappeared too. After a year his angina stopped completely and his cholesterol stabilized at two-thirds of its original level.

The problem with cardiovascular conditions is that they are often invisible in their early stages. Jennifer, a 69-year-old grandmother living alone, was concerned about her health. Ever since her doctor had diagnosed mild high blood pressure and given her diuretics and low-dose beta-blockers, she had been swimming every day, walking a lot and eating much less meat and more salads. However, she was worried about the side-effects of the beta-blockers and wanted to give them up if she could find a substitute. She began taking garlic in her food two to three times a day and tried not to eat so much instant food, her mainstay as she lived alone. Her doctor was unwilling to stop the pills but agreed to do it gradually, with frequent checks of her blood pressure. It became completely normal within six months. Her doctor was most surprised and took her off all medication.

Interestingly, garlic has recently been shown to be very effective in killing the amoeba organism that produces amoebic dysentery; it is as effective as metronidazole, the main drug currently used, at least in the laboratory. Professor Mirelman, of the Department of Parasitology at the Weizman Institute, Israel, believes that garlic could one day benefit the millions of amoebic dysentery sufferers around the world, not only because it has fewer side-effects than regular, modern drugs, but also because it is cheap and can be grown locally.

————Garlic can reduce blood sugar————

If animals are fed garlic and then given a lot of sugar, the amount of sugar in their blood falls far short of the expected peak. Garlic is able to reduce blood sugar levels and encourage the process that takes up the sugar in the blood and turns it into carbohydrate in the liver. It has been found that garlic increases the insulin which is in charge of the gathering up of excess sugar. This has been studied in animals with mild diabetes; the production of insulin was stimulated and sugar levels reduced by around 20 per cent, an effect equivalent to that of the anti-diabetic drug tolbutamide.

This does not make garlic a cure for diabetes. However, it might encourage people with pre-diabetes or a poor metabolizing of sugar to try garlic as a useful supplement to the diet.

————Garlic as a protection against————
cancer and poisons

The sulphur compounds in garlic are not unlike those in the body which act as the first defence against poisons. The liver uses such compounds to detoxify and disintegrate drugs, poisons and unwanted body chemicals.

In 1953, Dr Weissberger of Case Western University, Cleveland, Ohio, suggested that the sulphur in allicin might also protect against cancer by helping to remove cancer cells. He injected cancer cells into mice with or without a small amount of allicin from garlic. The mice who were injected with the cancer alone lived for only sixteen days, the others for six months.

This awakened some interest in the possibility of garlic as a preventive against cancer. Professor Sydney Belman of the New York Medical Centre found that onion and garlic oil were both able to prevent much of the expected cancer in mice injected with cancer-causing chemicals. Professor Michael Wargovich of the Department of Medical Oncology in the M.D. Anderson Hospital, Houston, Texas, recently found that he could prevent three-quarters of the expected, chemically-caused tumours by giving mice diallyl sulphide, one of the main constituents of garlic oil.

So far, the evidence from animal studies suggests that garlic may have a preventive or protective role against cancer. There is no evidence that it helps to treat it. Although it is not known whether garlic acts as a cancer preventive in people, an intriguing observation comes from China. Dr Mei Xing of Shandon Medical College observed that the people of Gangshan County had stomach cancer rates of 3.5 per 100,000 people. In the neighbouring Qixia county, the stomach cancer rates were more than ten times higher, at 40 per 100,000 people. The only thing he could find to account for the difference was that the people of Gangshan each ate on average about six cloves of garlic a day. Those from Qixia ate none.

Garlic's sulphur groups are also able to gather up toxic heavy metals in the body. One of the conventional treatments for heavy metal poisoning is to give cysteine, which is a sulphur-containing amino acid. In Bulgaria, a garlic preparation named Satal was used to help workers overcome industrial lead poisoning; it greatly reduced the symptoms of the poisoning and the amounts of heavy metals in the blood. Garlic can capture nearly its own weight of lead or mercury and, once bound, the metals can be eliminated. Another laboratory study with animals showed that garlic speeded up the elimination of the substances used in food additives.

Garlic in the garden

Bearing in mind that many readers will take the health of their gardens very much to heart, a few comments on the use of garlic against pests, worms and fungi in the garden would be appropriate although it is, strictly, outside our theme.

The agriculturalists of old used to plant garlic near their onions, cabbages and garden vegetables because it kept away various flies and grubs. Modern organic gardeners have found that garlic extract, highly diluted, kills or keep away wireworm, caterpillars, weevils and blackfly. The key to making a good garden concoction is to crush the garlic, leave it to generate its oily sulphides and then dilute it with water and oil-based soap. The active insect-killing materials are the sulphides in the oil. These are quite strong. Studies at the University of California have shown that mosquito larvae are killed by a dilution of one crushed clove in four litres of water.

Garlic is as useful against the fungi in the garden as it is in the body. Try it against mildew, beam rust, anthracnose, brown rot and blight.

CHAPTER 7

An open heart

The progress so far

The last two decades have seen a considerable improvement in the awareness of health. I remember twenty years ago going from bakery to bakery in the North of England looking for a good wholewheat loaf. Processed foods were the norm and anyone concerned about harmful food additives was regarded as an eccentric. The first vegetarian restaurant in London was deliberately named Cranks, as a play on the public image of vegetarians as sentimental faddists. Today, however, a great number of people know about the additives that are used in foods. Manufacturers are vying with each other to put 'natural' on their labels, even if it remains a questionable description of the contents. You can buy health food and even organically-grown foods in the supermarkets and cholesterol has become a household word.

For all that, we have a very long way to go. The reason that Britain has the highest rate of heart disease in the world is partly due to natural conservatism. In the UK, as in the USA and many modern countries, the food industry lobby, the dairy lobby, the meat lobby and the agricultural lobby have been very strong since the Second World War. They have certainly ensured that everyone has had enough to eat. However, efforts to simplify and clean up the diet have not got very far.

There is still a widespread assumption that heart disease is a misfortune which only affects some executives under stress, and that it is not worth worrying about unless your doctor tells you so. However, the doctors' function is curative, not preventive. Doctors have an extensive knowledge about what happens to the body if high blood pressure exists, and what drugs to use to depress it. However, little is taught at medical school about how to prevent it. That is left to the naturopaths, the health industry, books and magazines, with some marginal help from the health education authorities.

Modern medical treatments for cardiovascular disease come too little, too late. Strokes are considered to be more or less unpreventable. Heart by-pass operations, when coolly evaluated, have been shown to extend the lifespan only marginally, and only in severe cases, since the new vessels soon fur up like the one ones. Cardiac intensive care achieves little more than home treatment in a less stressed environment. Cardiovascular drugs introduce a range of side-effects that restrict the possible benefits. There are no panaceas, except prevention.

One of the excuses frequently given is that there is insufficient evidence for health authorities to make more radical naturopathic recommendations to the public. Even after hundreds of millions spent on research, it is said that the importance of lowering cholesterol is still not established. However, countries like Finland which have launched serious preventive programmes, regardless, have lowered their levels of heart disease dramatically. We cannot wait for interminable research projects. Prevention should start now. Research can, and will, confirm it later.

Garlic's popularity

Against this background, garlic has been one of the rediscoveries of the age. It has been taken in large quantities for many years to aid coughs, colds, catarrh, sore throats and other persistent infections. Now it is being brought into the limelight through its ability to help diseases of the circulation. There is so much evidence of its effects that it is becoming one of the most popular remedies in the modern world.

Garlic is a people's medicine. It is not a rare or special remedy, nor a pure drug with a patent on it, nor an expensive pharmaceutical concoction. Like all our herbal remedies and medicinal foods, it is part of our inheritance. With the growing movement towards herbs and natural remedies, our pharmacies are looking more and more like health shops and health shops are becoming a little like pharmacies. In France and Germany, especially, the latter now have a distinctly herbaceous atmosphere, more so than at any time since the days of the apothecaries. Garlic, as one of the most important preventive remedies known, naturally has an important place in this new movement.

The herbal tradition itself has gone through a major transition in the last few years, accompanying its rise in popularity. It is no longer full of old-fashioned, musty-smelling, peculiar remedies. Today herbalism is called *phytotherapy* and its herbs are often concentrated extracts prepared under scientifically controlled conditions and analysed in the laboratory to ensure purity and sufficient concentrations of the therapeutically active constituents. Herbs come in tablets and capsules, licensed by health authorities in a similar manner to pharmaceuticals. Garlic is a part of this revolution. As its popularity has increased, so has our knowledge of its effects and how to prepare and process it. We are beginning to benefit both from the experience of the past and from the modern research programmes.

Garlic and the medical establishment

Garlic is still not yet fully recognized by the medical establishments of all countries. Although no less than ten clinical trials were published during the years 1986–88, almost all on the cardiovascular effects, they were sufficient only to convince the health authorities in Germany, where most of them were carried out. There have been no serious clinical studies in the UK or the USA. Until this is done, the medical authorities there are unlikely to accept it fully or license it.

Although garlic oil has a licence from the authorities in the UK, this only allows manufacturers of garlic products to make claims of its effectiveness in relation to coughs, catarrh etc. This does not mean that garlic oil does not work as a cardiovascular preventive in Britain, only that the British health authorities are not yet convinced of it! They have not yet caught up with our full knowledge of garlic's effects. Until that happens, we are unlikely to find it in their National Health Service hospitals, either in the food or on the drugs trolley.

Nevertheless, it is likely that we will now see accelerated research programmes designed to find out exactly how strong garlic is as a cardiovascular preventative and how it compares with modern chemical drugs on the one hand and with other natural medicinal preparations such as MaxEPA on the other. We still do not really know how strong it is and what kinds of people will benefit most from it. There is also a need for more research on its anti-infective effects on humans, which would complement that already done in the laboratory.

The true place of natural remedies

For most of this century, we have been used to drugs. These are single chemical compounds with an exact and known action on a body processes. They are strong and specific. Their side-effects arise because their action on one particular part of the body can unleash unexpected changes elsewhere.

These drugs replaced the herbs which were the mainstay of all medicine before them. Herbs were deposed because they were regarded as unscientific, unreliable, weak and messy. Now that we know the problems which drugs cause, there is a renewal of interest in herbal remedies. We find that most of them were removed from the pharmacopoeiae without any rational justification. They were not dismissed because they were useless, since their effectiveness was never tested in the laboratory.

Now that herbs are returning to our medicine-chest, we should ask ourselves whether the original criticism were true or not. They turn out to have been true only from a medical perspective which diagnoses a precise set of symptoms and then uses specific drugs to eradicate them. A more traditional, natural or 'complementary' approach is to reduce the vulnerability or susceptibility to the disease and encourage the body to throw it off by itself. Herbs fit very well into this approach. They often have effects which are adjustive, which work with the body rather than against it. For example, herbs like Echinacea, yarrow or liquorice can support and encourage the body's immunity and help it throw off an infection. No present-day drug is able to achieve such an effect. Garlic, likewise, is able to prevent diseases of the circulation in a way unmatched by any modern medicine. Common herbs such as mint, comfrey, coltsfoot, feverfew and thousands of others can deal with symptoms without upsetting the *vix mediatrix naturae*, the natural healing process.

Herbs are, it is true, weaker than pure chemicals and do not dispose of symptoms so fast. However, they are more gentle and keep closer to the original medical maxim, 'First do no harm'. Their weakness can be a disadvantage if you have a runaway and serious infection. On the other hand a herb can affect a range of processes which otherwise would require a whole battery of drugs. We have seen this in the cardiovascular system where garlic affects blood clotting, cholesterol, and thinness of the blood, as well as its other useful effects such as getting rid of extra body water and lowering blood pressure.

These properties make herbs irreplaceable in prevention and in the self-treatment of many minor or chronic problems. Whether or not you wish to use them for more serious conditions will depend to a large extent on professional advice. Herbs can be used for virtually all health problems, either alone or with other forms of treatment. However, expert advice will enable you to get the best from them and this should always be sought when dealing with serious illnesses.

──────The limits of self-care──────

Three-quarters of all health problems never arrive in the doctor's waiting room. Most of them are mild and self-limiting, that is to say they pass away by themselves, and are dealt with in daily life. For every episode of chest pain that is caused by angina, there will be thousands that are due to a passing tightness in the muscles.

In other words, people mostly look after themselves. Mild remedies like garlic or other herbs or vitamins are helpful in this because they provide the tools of self-care. However, their true effectiveness depends on how much you know. The more you know about garlic, for example, the less you will find yourself at the doctor's surgery asking for an antibiotic. In the modern world a great deal of this knowledge has been lost. We have been encouraged to take all our problems to the expert, who will deal with them without even telling us what he is doing. Indeed, given the strength of modern drugs, it is a good thing that we do not treat ourselves with them. But because of this general lack of knowledge, we start at a disadvantage. The only way to overcome this is to learn. That is why so many health books are both written and read. It is a process of re-learning about the natural medicines all around us.

Nevertheless, for the proper treatment of any medical condition by herbs and diet, you would be well advised to seek professional advice. This does not mean that you cannot help yourself; it means that you might achieve better results if your efforts were monitored and guided by a professional. In the case of the heart and circulatory system, it would be as well to have occasional check-ups. If everything is satisfactory, then you do not need professional help in treatment. However, you may still appreciate some advice on a regimen of general health maintenance to suit your personal situation. If your professional advisor finds that you are potentially vulnerable to cardiovascular problems, he may be able to design a regimen that will be more effective than your own. For example, he may recommend certain herbs to take along with garlic, or he may review your diet with you.

The professionals who are best able to work with you in this way are naturopaths, herbalists, and many homoeopaths or holistic doctors. Conventional doctors who do not have a holistic training are not so adept. However, with the rise of complementary medicine there are more experts able to assist your efforts.

There remains the question of how one should take in and use all the information now available on health care. This is the second book I have written on garlic and each time people have asked me how it is possible to write a whole book on the subject. I reply, quoting William Blake, that it is possible to see a world in a grain of sand. However, as far as health is concerned, there is so much advice and information today, in the form of hundreds of books, articles and commercial material, that it is not possible for everyone to be an expert on all the regimes, remedies and supplements.

Instead, I would suggest a different approach. Concentrate on learning about yourself, noticing your body and observing your general condition, just like the careful car owner who knows how to listen to his engine and always seems to have his vehicle on the road when all the rest have broken down. Then it will become clear to you which are the essential self-care tools you need. With its wide applicability, long tradition of reliable use and great safety, garlic will surely be one of them.

CHAPTER 8

Products and preparations: How to take garlic

Garlic is as effective as a medicine as some modern drugs. It can thin the blood more efficiently than the other favourite, a little aspirin every day. It can reduce the build-up of fats in the circulation as well as, or better than, cholestyramine, a drug used for this purpose which is not completely safe. Garlic's anti-infective properties may be as good as those of the modern antifungal drugs.

Garlic, however, is different in that it is a plant and a natural food-medicine. Unlike drugs, garlic is non-toxic and is therefore completely safe to take regularly. It is not a pill containing a precise amount of pure chemical, to be swallowed unthinkingly twice a day. It requires more attention from you. You will need to know how much to take, and the most effective way of taking it for your particular purposes. It is important to understand the different garlic products available on the market so that you can choose the one that best suits you. According to your own preferences, you will need to know the various ways of reducing the smell. This sounds a lot to take in. However, perhaps one should apply the same kind of consideration to any plant, whether you use it as a food or a medicine. To get the best from garlic, get involved with it. You will find a special fun in knowing your subject thoroughly — and your cooking will benefit too.

The dosage of garlic

For all preventive purposes, including the protection of the circulation, you should take at least one clove of garlic, weighing from 2 to 3 grams, a day. This is the minimum dose; we will call it the *preventive dose*. It is advisable to take some at least twice a day, as studies have shown that it stays in the body and circulation for just a few hours before it is removed or neutralized. Therefore it is necessary to take at least one to one and a half grams (or half a clove) morning and evening.

There are situations where you will need to take much more than this. When you use garlic to treat a disease or a symptom - bronchial and throat problems, stomach infections, skin infections and so on - then a *therapeutic dose* is required. The reason is that you need a much more powerful punch to knock out bacteria, yeasts or fungi, than to inhibit cholesterol, fats and blood clots in the circulation. The therapeutic dose should be a minimum of a clove's worth (2-3g) three times a day. This is the amount suggested in the British Herbal Pharmacopoeia, from traditional sources and modern herbal guides. In my own experience it is the minimum needed to maintain a real antiseptic/antibiotic action in the body tissues. For those who rarely touch garlic, it may seem a lot. However, it is really not so large a dose: in many societies, in parts of China, for example, people would eat this much or more in their diet on a regular basis, children included.

The therapeutic dose is not normally required in order to look after your circulation. However, there are situations where it is advisable to take this dose. If you have had or are having a very heavy or fatty meal, or where you suspect the wholesomeness of the food, it would be worth neutralising it with one or two cloves of garlic. Again, in more serious cases of circulatory disease or atherosclerosis, garlic may be used as part of a therapeutic programme in order to regain health.

Very occasionally, and unusually, it may be necessary to take very large doses indeed, a whole bulb, or head of garlic or more. This is what we would call a *saturation dose*. This would occur where more serious infections such as abscesses, dysentery or septic wounds, were developing and you were unable or unwilling to take modern drugs.

Taking fresh garlic

Fresh garlic should be taken either with a quantity of warm water or milk, with fruit such as apples and pears, with vegetable juices and soups, or with green salads such as lettuce and parsley. All of these methods will help to eliminate the burning sensation in mouth or stomach. The green leafy salads, especially parsley, will also reduce the subsequent familiar aroma.

Fresh garlic is still medicinally effective if eaten with food. However, the body may not be able to absorb all the garlic if it is taken with a full meal, so it is advisable to increase the amount.

Here are some more detailed ways of taking fresh garlic that you might like to try:

1. Garlic in milk or yogurt
Crush a clove in half a cup of warm milk (goat's milk if preferred). Add honey to taste. This is an old gypsy remedy. As milk is not the best drink to take when there are chest or throat infections, or where there is mucus, this remedy can be modified by substituting kumiss or yoghurt.

2. Garlic syrup
This is similar to the garlic syrups described in the official drug guides, such as the British Pharmacopoeia, earlier this century. It is recommended by many herbalists as a handy and effective medicine-chest item, ready when needed. The garlic is not fresh as in the other recipes, and some of the allicin will have decayed, yet it seems to keep its power remarkably well.

Put 250g of crushed garlic in a 1-litre jar. Almost fill with cider vinegar and water, cover and leave for a few days, shaking occasionally. Strain through a cloth, add 1 cup of honey, stir and keep in the fridge. One tablespoon three times a day will give the correct dose. It is especially useful for coughs, nasal and bronchial problems and sore throats, as well as for circulatory problems.

3. Garlic and miso soup
Miso, or Japanese soybean extract, makes an excellent hot soup, ideal to take with garlic. Dissolve a teaspoonful of miso in just-boiled water. Add a couple of drips of soy sauce, a good squeeze of lemon, some grated onion and the crushed clove of garlic. This is especially good during the convalescent period of an infection, as it brings strength as well as healing. At a pinch, a concentrated vegetable stock can be substituted for the miso.

4. External applications: fresh garlic on the skin
There are occasions, for example athlete's foot, fungal infections, stings, Candida in the urogenital area, or tooth and gum infections, where garlic needs to be applied to the skin or mucosal surfaces. If the skin is not overly sensitive, one can simply crush garlic onto a small piece of lint, place it on the area and bind it. There may be some burning sensation, which passes in a few minutes. The garlic can be kept to the required area by spreading petroleum jelly on the surrounding parts.

If the burning would otherwise be too intense, for example on the gums, one can use a slice of garlic which has been left for 30 minutes after crushing.

How to deal with the odour

Garlic's strong odour comes mostly from the sulphides and disulphides which are formed by the natural changes in the allicin.

When you eat fresh garlic, the immediate odour arises from the mouth and the teeth; some more comes from the stomach and the rest from the lungs and skin. You can substantially reduce the mouth odour by swallowing the garlic quickly without chewing it, by washing it down with liquid, or by making a 'pill' with lettuce or parsley.

Lettuce, parsley, aromatic seeds such as aniseed, mint and cloves all reduce and disguise the odours from the stomach. These should be eaten with, and after, the garlic. The odour from the skin and lungs cannot be avoided; however, it is milder.

The major way to reduce the odour, however, is undoubtedly to use one or other garlic product available on the market (see below). Some of these employ very interesting modern methods of reducing and virtually eliminating the odour.

───────────Fried and cooked garlic───────────

If garlic is crushed in a frying pan, some allicin is produced immediately and then the heat of the cooking converts it to the oily and strongly odorous sulphides and disulphides. Fried or cooked garlic is therefore the equivalent of the garlic oil in the capsules which we will discuss next. It is made by a process that includes steaming. Fried or cooked garlic is therefore an effective medicine.

───────────Garlic products───────────

As we have seen, garlic products have become extremely popular in the last few years. They provide an opportunity to share in the undoubted health benefits of garlic without incurring the penalties.

Their main popularity has naturally been in Northern Europe and in the USA, where garlic is not yet a national flavour. There are, however, many products, from the comparatively odorous to the completely sanitized and deodorized. These are oils, powders, extracts, pills and capsules. How effective are they? Which ones are best? One can divide the products into three main groups.

Garlic oil capsules

Garlic oil is the essential or aromatic oil of garlic. It is made by mashing it in a big vat, and then bubbling steam through it. The oily components are carried through on the steam and then collected once the steam has cooled. Another way of making garlic oil is to add a large quantity of vegetable oil to garlic mash in a vat without any heating. The vegetable oil takes up the garlic oil, after which the solids are removed by filtration. This is called an oil macerate and is used in some European oil capsules.

The oil of garlic is formed when its allicin decays naturally to create the oily sulphides, disulphides, trisulphides and other compounds. In ordinary fresh garlic, or in fresh garlic mixed with vegetable oil, this change happens over a few days. When garlic mash is steam-distilled, it happens immediately, as it does when garlic is fried.

Garlic oil is therefore very similar to fried garlic. The amount of the oil is roughly the same as the amount of allicin which produced it, that is to say from 0.1% to 0.2 per cent of the total weight. In other words, at least ½-1 ton of fresh garlic gives 1kg of oil. This makes it extremely concentrated. One clove weighing 2-3 grams would have in it 2-6 milligrams (or thousandths of a gram) of the oil.

Garlic oil is normally sold in capsules, in which a very small amount is suspended in vegetable oil and enclosed in gelatine. These capsules were the very first product. They were developed in the 1920s by Dr Hofels in Germany and described as garlic perles. They have been consistently popular for the last 60 years. In fact, most of the 300 million doses of garlic consumed in the UK last year were in the form of garlic oil perles. Most of them were made by Hofels, the company which Dr Hofels founded.

Garlic oil perles have an obvious advantage in that they are swallowed whole and therefore avoid completely the mouth odour that comes from chewing. The contents themselves have a strong garlic odour. This is released in the stomach and some emerges again on the breath. Moreover, the odour of some capsules has been reduced even further by giving them a coating which does not dissolve in the stomach. They pass through it and dissolve in the intestine, thus avoiding the 'repeating' that is usual with ordinary capsules.

But are these capsules effective? There have been a number of studies on this question. It has been found by scientists like Professor Bordia, a pioneer of garlic research in India, and Dr Qureshi, of the United States Department of Agriculture, that the oil is as effective as fresh garlic at reducing cholesterol and blood clotting, and as a general cardiovascular preventive. Thus, the popularity of garlic perles over the years has been confirmed in the laboratory.

Studies have shown that fresh garlic or garlic juice which is placed in the middle of a 'sea' of bacteria will kill all those within a distance of several centimetres. If garlic oil is used, the power to kill the bacteria or fungi is much reduced, though it is still present. Thousands of people have borne witness to the help given by garlic perles with their coughs and sore throats, and the government has given a licence allowing garlic oil capsules to be advertised for catarrh, coughs etc.

We have seen that one clove of garlic will produce 2-6mg of oil. This is a daily 'preventive' dose. Most perles on the market today contain less than 1mg of oil, 0.66mg being the most popular. The reason in part is that this is the traditional dosage, set in the dim and distant past. It is the dose acknowledged by the UK Ministry of Health in its licence and this encourages manufacturers to stick to it. Yet one will need 2-9 such perles per day to achieve the minimum preventive dose and 16-30 perles per day to achieve the therapeutic dose corresponding to 3 cloves.

In fact, a number of researchers, such as Dr Sampson of the Edinburgh Royal Infirmary, have carried out such studies on patients using the oil capsules. It turned out that when oil that is freshly prepared in the laboratory is used, the thinning of the blood and the reducing of cholesterol can be clearly demonstrated. But when some oil capsules were used according to the manufacturers' recommendations, no results were obtained. These oil capsules were of the low dose type. We can now see that the studies failed through inadequate dosage, a conclusion agreed by the researchers.

Fortunately, one leading company, Hofels, has understood the problem and now offers capsules containing 4mg of an oil which has been specially treated to keep it fresh. One in the morning would make up a preventive dose and 2-3 taken throughout the day would provide a therapeutic dose. They are also coated in such a way that the oil is released in the intestine, so controlling the odour.

Dried garlic powder products

Another way of concentrating garlic and making it into a pharmaceutical product is by drying it. Garlic is nearly two-thirds water, so if you dry it you produce a powder which is then ready to put in capsules or tablets. These can then be coated to reduce the aroma. Potentially this is a good way of preserving medicinal qualities, since it is possible to achieve high levels of allicin in such powders.

It sounds very simple, but is in fact very complicated. Special conditions are necessary in order to produce the maximum amounts of allicin and active ingredients in the dried powder. For example, if the garlic is ground and dried very quickly, there will be no time for it to make allicin; you will get a more or less odourless and less effective powder. On the other hand, if it is prepared slowly, the allicin will alter spontaneously to produce the oily compounds and not much will have been gained. This is the case with the dried garlic used in food. The food industry dries a great deal of garlic into powder, flakes and granules. The drying uses higher temperatures and longer times, with the result that the allicin is lost. Even the oil content is minimal, due to processing and long storage. For these reasons the dried garlic powder or granules you find in the supermarket is not suitable as a medicine. Nor can you expect much in the way of therapeutic value from the garlic in processed products.

The powders can therefore vary from very good to very poor. This presents a problem for the consumer, who has a right to know the potency of any product. Fortunately there are two tests which can be made to assess whether or not the powder contains high levels of allicin. One you can do yourself, one the manufacturer must do.

1. The taste test
Allicin is pungent and burning; however, it does not have a heavy odour. The oily sulphides, on the other hand, have the typically rich, heavy, clinging, sulphurous aroma of garlic, but do not have a burning taste. So you can test the contents of a pill or capsule by taste. Firstly it should be *strong*, otherwise it will be no good at all. Secondly it should have *both* the burning taste of allicin (the more the better) *and* the rich aroma of the sulphides.

2. The analytic test
It is now possible to analyse garlic extracts and products by a technique called High Pressure Liquid Chromatography (HPLC). This will tell the chemist exactly how much alliin and allicin there is in the product, and how much of the other components. This is quite a recent development; it only became possible to do it in 1987 after some new analytic methods developed in Germany were published. From now on, manufacturers will have no excuse for not stating the allicin content of their powdered products. Look for products which state the allicin content on the packaging.

If the powder is made very well indeed, it should be equally effective as the best product available. It will be equally effective as an anti-infective, for the protection of the circulation and in the other areas where garlic is useful.

This is an areas of active research. In China, Europe and the USA, efforts are being made to produce the perfect garlic powder extract for medicinal use. In particular, efforts are being made to discover ways of preserving allicin in dry powders. This is very difficult to do and has not been achieved yet. However, we can expect some interesting new developments in the future.

CHAPTER 9

—A brief history of garlic—

This book has dealt principally with the present day, with the modern research which has been carried out on garlic and what it can do to help in the current epidemic of heart disease. The situation is urgent, the possibilities dramatic and the scientific justification and backing for them far more substantial than the majority of people realize. So we have not dealt much on the details of garlic's past, though it has a fascinating one, both as a food and a medicine.

Mankind and garlic have had a long and passionate relationship. Garlic, in its cultivated form, needs man to ensure its propagation. But just as much, man has needed garlic to guard his health, well-being and vigour. Dig up the past and you'll find it everywhere. Little clay models of garlic bulbs were found in a 6000 year old Egyptian burial ground at El Mahasana. The tomb of King Tutankhamun himself contained six dried bulbs: perhaps they were there to provide him with essential sustenance during his long journey through the nether worlds. The Egyptians clearly appreciated garlic both as an enrichment of the diet and also as an important medicine. A 3500 year old Egyptian medical text, the Ebers Papyrus, lists twenty-two garlic recipes for problems such as stomach infections, boils, bodily weaknesses and infected glands.

Garlic was the fare of ancient kings and was relied on for taste, strength and nourishment by the common folk. The Jews in the Wilderness, so the Bible says (Numbers 11: 4-6), became so bored with their monotonous diet of manna that they longed for the garlicky food of Egypt, even though they had eaten it as slaves. The ancient Greeks loved their garlic and Aristotle recommended it as a tonic. The Romans, too, were typically Mediterranean in their appreciation. Virgil praised its restorative power for reapers during the long, hot harvest. Their legionaries planted it wherever they were stationed, in vegetable plots beyond the walls of their camps. They believed that it made them fighting fit and more aggressive. Indeed the Roman wish, 'May you not eat garlic', was the equivalent of saying, 'May you not receive your call-up papers'.

Throughout history garlic has been valued as a medicine as well as a food. Hippocrates, who lived on the Greek island of Kos and is the distant forefather of modern medicine, praised garlic for driving out excess water from the body, for settling upset stomachs and for curing infections and inflammations. This is one of his remedies for an infected lung:

'. . . And if you recognise the signs of suppuration, the sick man, for his evening meal and before he goes to bed, should eat raw garlic in great quantity and should drink a noble and pure wine. If by this means the pus erupts, so much the better.'

Dioscorides, the Roman physician whose understanding of plants has been the inspiration of herbalists right up to the present day, had this to say about it:

'Garlic . . . makes the voice clear and soothes continuous coughing when eaten raw or boiled. Boiled with oregano, it kills lice and bed bugs. It clears the arteries. Burnt and mixed with honey, it is an ointment for bloodshot eyes; it also helps baldness. Together with salt and oil, it heals eczema. Together with honey, it heals white spots, herpetic eruptions, liver spots, leprosy and scurvy. Boiled with pine-wood and incense, it soothes tooth-ache when the solution is kept in the mouth. Garlic with fig leaves and cumin is a plaster against the biting of the shrew-mouse . . . A mush from crushed garlic and black olives is a diuretic. It is helpful in dropsy.'

Galen, one of the true fathers of medicine, called it the countryman's cure-all (*theriacum rusticorum*) and Gaius Pliny, the greatest natural historian of ancient times, compiled an astonishing list of up to fifty disorders which it would cure. Pliny died observing the eruption of Vesuvius which buried Pompeii – in whose ashes garlic was, of course, found preserved.

The Romans presumably brought garlic with them to England, where it became valued as a flavouring for goose. Throughout mediaeval and Renaissance Europe, it was a familiar part of life and its smell was a part of its fun. A contemporary source mentions how Henry IV of France (1566-93) chewed garlic and had 'a breath that would fell an ox at twenty paces'. At the same time its health-giving qualities were praised by all leading herbalists. By their theory of elements and humours, it was regarded as very 'heating' and 'drying' and was therefore used to combat 'moist' and 'cold' diseases, including catarrh and boils, various stubborn infections and sluggish circulation of the blood. According to Queen Elizabeth's herbalist, Wiliam Turner, it 'maketh subtill the nourishment and the blood', implying that it cleared blockages in both. This statement is of course of great interest to us today.

However, as long ago as 1600 a prejudice against garlic's pungency as a food developed in northern, Protestant Europe. It came to be regarded as the food of rustics and peasants, but not suited to the refined palates of the upper classes. This is shown in Shakespeare, in *Measure for Measure*. Act III, Scene ii, where Lucio says of the Duke that he would 'mouth with a beggar though she smell brown bread and garlic'. In 1699, in his book on salads, the famous diarist John Evelyn wrote of garlic, 'We absolutely forbid it entrance into our salleting by reason of its intolerable rankness'. Spaniards, Italians and French people might eat it, so might countrymen, especially if they lived in damp places, and sailors, but not English ladies and gentlemen. During the nineteenth century this distaste was well expressed by the culinary and domestic 'guru', Mrs Beeton. As she wrote in her *Book of Household Management*, 'The smell of this plant is generally considered offensive . . . It was in greater repute with our ancestors than it is with ourselves, although it is still used as a seasoning or herb.'

The dislike spread with the Anglo-Saxons to the United States of America, where a poll conducted not long ago on the subject of tastes found that garlic was the most unpopular flavour of all, along with olive oil. At the top of the list were, of course, banana, chocolate and strawberries.

This prejudice is in part still with us and must be taken seriously. How did it arise? To judge by the various cutting remarks in Shakespeare, it arose because aristocratic people began to express their refinement through a new, starched cleanliness. Pungent smells became the province of the poor; for the rich it was all lavender and roses. As the process continued, bland tastes and odours became associated with self-discipline, primness and restraint. Garlic was associated with the forbidden passions indulged in by Mediterranean peoples and with the repellent grubbiness of the working classes.

Now the change is coming about. Today it is the middle and upper class, health conscious trend-setters who eat garlic, along with brown, whole-wheat bread and other natural foods. The old bland, inoffensive cooking is seen as inhibited and unhealthy, as well as unnecessary. The return to a natural lifestyle is accompanied by an acceptance of natural smells.

────────Garlic as a traditional medicine────────

Let us look more closely at garlic as a traditional medicine. The language and practice of the old herbals can seem picturesque and confusing if one does not know how to extract the essential truth and common sense contained there. This is particularly the case with garlic as it appears to have such a bewildering array of uses. Nevertheless, once these are summarized under rational and consistent headings the by now familiar picture emerges. These are as follows:

Against infections

Garlic was especially recommended by herbalists in infections of the stomach (e.g. dysentery), mouth, throat (e.g. sore throat, coughs, catarrh), ears and skin. It was used both internally and externally for boils, spots, carbuncles and ulcers. During the First World War it was extensively used by both sides to treat infected wounds. In the British trenches, sterilized sphagnum moss containing garlic juice was generally placed over the injury. Reports from that time describe it as a successful front-line protection against gangrene. It was also used in the trenches against dysentery, a practice continued during the Second World War by the countries of Eastern Europe.

Garlic has been used against some very ugly infections indeed. Saturation doses were used, with some effectiveness, to treat tuberculosis and leprosy, something which still continues in remote areas of the world. It was also used against cholera and typhoid, with considerable success according to medical and popular records. Dr Albert Schweitzer certainly used it in this way in Africa. Even the plague, while not cured by garlic, may have been deterred by it: French priests who attended the bedsides of victims in eighteenth-century London remained healthy, while the non-garlic eating English priests succumbed.

Bites, stings and poisons

Garlic is widely spoken of as the foremost first aid remedy against the assaults of the more unpleasant side of the animal kingdom. Aristotle recommended it for the bites of mad dogs, Mohammed for scorpion stings; the author can personally vouch for the latter in the case of a certain common, non-lethal but unpleasant Middle Eastern scorpion. Greek and Roman herbalists called it an antidote to snakebite and told how farmers would carry it with them in the fields as an emergency remedy.

There were other anti-toxic effects, the most famous being its ability to deal with a hangover. In France the recommended 'morning after' cure was a soup made of onions and garlic.

Other miscellaneous uses

Garlic was used to treat tumours and growths on the skin, and also scurvy. Rheumatism and piles are also mentioned. Some of these various used probably relied on garlic's ability to heat the body, so causing sweating and cleansing.

It was also used to control infestation of intestinal worms in men and animals, still an extremely important effect in poorer parts of the world, and it is supposed to deter fleas and lice from biting.

The circulation

Garlic clears the arteries, said Dioscorides, as did William Turner after him, and it was consistently used to cure 'blockages' or 'stiffness' of the blood system. Arising from poor circulation was the relatively common disease 'dropsy', in which parts or all of the body swelled up and became waterlogged, a condition we would now call oedema. Garlic was the principal treatment for this. In Asian, and especially Indian, medicine garlic was specifically used to remove fat from the blood and dry out excess moisture from the body. (By the same token they noted that it reduced the amount of milk produced by breast-feeding mothers and they recommended them to be careful of their consumption). Charaka, the traditional father of Indian medicine, states that garlic maintains the fluidity of the blood and strengthens the heart, and traditional Indian physicians nowadays rely on garlic and onion 'lasona' therapy to prevent heart disease.

The traditional explanation of how garlic 'maketh subtill the blood' tells us that the old herbalists really understood something of how it achieves this important effect. It resulted, they said, from garlic's heating and drying properties, which removed water from the body and opened 'cold', atrophied and blocked blood vessels. Today, of course, we would call the condition of these blocked vessels atherosclerosis and speak of degenerative diseases of the circulation, which means much the same thing. The use of garlic in circulatory problems has been the main theme of this book. Here we see that it has an ancient precedent.

Further reading

Books on garlic

Blackwood, J. and Fulder, S. *Garlic, Nature's Original Remedy* Javelin Books, Cassells, London (1986).

Koch, H.P., and Hahn, G. *Knoblauch* Urban and Scharzenberg, Munich (1988).

Harris, L. *The Book of Garlic* Panjandrum/Aris, Los Angeles (1979).

Books on garlic cookery

Shulman, M.R. *Garlic Cookery* Thorsons, Wellingborough (1984).

Drinkwater, P. and Self, E. *A Passion for Garlic* Duckworths, London (1984).

Selected scientific references

Garlic chemistry

Block, E. 'The Chemistry of Garlic and Onions' *Scientific American*, 252, 94–97 (1985).

Brodnitz, M. H. et al. 'Flavour Components of Garlic Extract' *J. of Agricultural Food Chemistry*, 19, 273–275 (1971).

Fenwick, G.R. and Hanley, A.B. 'The Genus *Allium*' Parts 1-3, *Critical Reviews on Food Science*, Vols 22 and 23 (1986).

Garlic's effects on the circulation

Apitz-Castro, R. et al. 'Ajoene, the Antiplatelet Principle of Garlic' *Thrombosis Research*, 42, 303–311 (1986).

Banerjee, A.K. 'Effect of Aqueous Extract of Garlic on Arterial Blood Pressure of Normotensive and Hypertensive Rats' *Artery*, 2, 369–373 (1976).

Bordia, A. et al. 'Effects of the Essential Oils of Garlic and Onion on Alimentary Hyperlipidaemia' *Atherosclerosis*, 21, 15–19 (1975).

Bordia, A. and Verma, S.K. 'Effect of Garlic Feeding on Regression of Experimental Atherosclerosis in Rabbits' *Artery*, 7, 428–437 (1980).

Bordia, A. 'Effect of Garlic on Blood Lipids in Patients with Coronary Heart Disease' *American J. Clinical Nutrition*, 34, 200–203 (1981).

Boullin, D.J. 'Garlic as a Platelet Inhibitor' *Lancet*, 1, 776–777 (1981).

Chi, M.S. et al. 'Effects of Garlic on Lipid Metabolism in Rats Fed Cholesterol or Lard' *J. Nutrition*, 112, 41–48 (1982).

Chutani, S.K. and Bordia, A. 'The Effect of Fried Versus Raw Garlic on Fibrinolytic Activity in Man' *Atherosclerosis*, 38, 417–421 (1981).

De Boer, L.W.V. and Folts, J.D. 'Garlic Extracts Limit Acute Platelet Thrombus Formation in the Canine Coronary Arteries' *Clinic Research*, 34, 292A (1986).

Ernst, E. et al. 'Garlic and Blood Lipids' *British Medical Journal*, 291, 139 (1985).

Ernst, E. 'Cardiovascular Effects of Garlic (*Allium sativum*): A Review' *Pharmatherapeutica*, 5, 83–89 (1987).

Editorial, 'Natural Fibrinolysis and its Stimulation' *Lancet*, 1, 1401–1402 (1982).

Foushee, D.B. et al. 'Garlic as a Natural Agent for the Treatment of Hypertension: a Preliminary Report' *Cytobios*, 34, 145–152 (1982).

Activity of Blood' *Am. J. Clinical Nutrition*, 30, 1380–1381 (1977).

Kandziora, J. 'Antihypertensive Wirksamkeit und Verträghchkeit eines Knoblauch-Präparates' *Ärtzliche Forschung*, 35, 1–8 (1988).

Keyes, A. 'Wine, Garlic and CHD in Seven Countries' *Lancet*, 145–146 (1980).

König, F.K. and Schneider, B. 'Knoblauch Bessert Derchbluntungsstörungen *Ärztliche Praxis*, 38, 344–345 (1986).

Makheja, A.N. et al. 'Inhibition of Platelet Aggregation and Thromboxane Synthesis by Onion and Garlic' *Lancet*, 781 (1979).

Sainani, B.S. et al. 'Effect of Dietary Garlic and Onion on Serum Lipid Profile in a Jain community' *Indian J. Med. Research*, 69, 776–780 (1979).

Srivastava, K.C. 'Evidence for the Mechanism by Which Garlic Inhibits Platelet Aggregation' *Prostagl. Leukotr. M.*, 22, 313–321 (1986).

Zhao, F. et al. 'Study of Synthetic Allicin on the prevention and treatment of Atherosclerosis' *Yingyang Xuebao*, 3, 109–116 (1982).

Garlic against infections

Caporaso, L. et al. 'Antifungal Activity in Human Urine and Serum After Ingestion of Garlic (*Allium sativum*)' *Antimicrobiol. Agric. Chem.* 23, 700–702 (1983).

Mirelman, D. et al. 'Inhibition of Growth of Entamoeba Histolytica by Allicin, the Active Principle of Garlic Extract' *J. Infectious Diseases*, 156, 243–244 (1987).

Moore, G.S. and Atkins, R.D. 'Fungicidal and Fungistatic Effects of an Aqueous Garlic Extract on Medically Important Yeast-Like Fungi' *Mycologia*, 69, 341–348.

Adetumbi, M.A. and Lau, B.H.S. '*Allium sativum* (garlic) - A Natural

Antibiotic' *Medical Hypotheses*, 12, 227–237 (1983).

Amer, M. et al. 'The Effect of Aqueous Garlic Extract on the Growth of Dermatophytes' *Internat. J. of Dermatol.*, 19, 285–287 (1980).

Garlic and blood sugar

Augusti, K.T. 'Studies on the Effect of Allicin (diallyl-disulphide-oxide) on Alloxan Diabetes' *Experientia*, 31, 1263–1265 (1975).

Chang, M.L.W. and Johnson, M.A. 'Effect of Garlic on Carbohydrate Metabolism and Lipid Synthesis in Rats' *J. Nutrition*, 110, 931–936 (1980).

Jain, R.C. et al. 'Hypoglycaemic Action of Onion and Garlic'. *Lancet*, 1491 (1973).

Garlic and Tumour Prevention

Weisberger, H.S. and Pensky, J. 'Tumour-Inhibiting Effects Derived from an Active Principle of Garlic (Allium sativum)' *Science*, 126, 1112–1114 (1957).

Belman, S. 'Onion and Garlic Oils and Tumour Promotion' *Carcinogenesis*, 4, 1063–1065 (1983).

Wargovich, M.J. 'Diallyl sulphide, a Flavour Component of Garlic (*Allium sativum*), Inhibits Dimethylhydrazine Induced Colon Cancer' *Carcinogenesis*, 8, 487–489 (1987).

Index